Praise for
You Are More Than Your Body

"In *You Are More Than Your Body*, Dr. Jennifer Caspari combines her clinical expertise with her lived experience to create a must-read guide for anyone looking to live their life with more ease. [The book] feels like a conversation with a wise, kind, and loving friend in which Dr. Caspari effortlessly integrates evidence-based psychological strategies with personal narrative to enable the reader to shift their mindset and make meaningful changes in their life."

—ALEXIS CONASON, PsyD, CEDS-C, clinical psychologist, Certified Eating Disorder Specialist, and author of *The Diet-Free Revolution*

"Written from a place of honest vulnerability, *You Are More Than Your Body* shares an accessible roadmap to self-acceptance and is a guide from which everyone can benefit."

—SHARON SALZBERG, author of *Lovingkindness* and *Real Life*

"Dr. Jennifer Caspari stands at the unique intersection of being a highly skilled psychologist and a woman with a disability. From this vantage point, she offers us a profoundly compassionate and practical guide to enhancing our well-being . . . a must-read for anyone looking to navigate life's challenges with an open mind and determined heart."

—DR. DIANA HILL, clinical psychologist, host of the *Wise Effort* podcast, and author of *The Self-Compassion Daily Journal*

"With warmth, honesty, and mature professional insight, Dr. Caspari shares her personal journey of life with cerebral palsy, providing readers with a guidebook for emotional and psychological resilience. I strongly recommend it for anyone seeking to transform their personal challenges into growth opportunities."

—KENT DRESCHER, PhD, clinical psychologist living with muscular dystrophy and coauthor of *The Moral Injury Workbook*

"Understanding your own worth and value is the greatest gift you can give yourself and others. Dr. Jennifer Caspari has written a beautiful guide to support you on your journey and help you accept and love yourself even more."

—SHANNON KAISER, best-selling author of *The Self-Love Experiment*

"The book so many of my patients need. Written with the authority of a clinical psychologist and expert in coping with disability/chronic illness, as well as with the knowledge and compassion of someone who has lived these experiences, what Dr. Caspari shares will resonate deeply with those who have felt different or limited by their bodies and provide hope to those who have felt alone in their struggles. Just as importantly, she shares a toolbox of evidence-based approaches for regulating emotions, shaping thoughts, and caring for your body, which come together to reset your relationship with your chronic health condition or disability and allow you to thrive."

—DR. JADE WU, author of *Hello Sleep: The Science and Art of Overcoming Insomnia Without Medications*

"A compassionate guide for anyone with a chronic health condition—offering hope and a practical path to thriving. Through personal stories and insights, it acknowledges the complexity of difficult experiences while providing clear psychological strategies for tolerating discomfort and managing thoughts and emotions. It's a must-read for anyone seeking greater self-acceptance and empowerment."

—ANNA KRESS, PsyD, licensed clinical psychologist and author of *Heal Your Past to Manifest Your Future*

"Reading *You Are More Than Your Body* feels like sitting down with a great friend—one who shares her story with authenticity, humor, and eye-opening common sense. Dr. Jennifer Caspari offers not just coping skills but also powerful principles to guide each of us on our unique journeys. Keep a notebook handy. Don't just read her book; capture these tools and practice them—they will empower you as you navigate life's inevitable messiness and challenges."

—STEPHANIE SZOSTAK, actor and author of *SELF!SH*

YOU ARE MORE THAN YOUR BODY

YOU ARE MORE THAN YOUR BODY

30+ Evidence-Based
Strategies for Living Well
with Chronic Illness

Jennifer
Caspari, PhD

North Atlantic Books
Huichin, unceded Ohlone land
Berkeley, California

North Atlantic Books   Cover design by Amanda Weiss
Huichin, unceded Ohlone land   Book design by Happenstance Type-O-Rama
2526 Martin Luther King Jr Way
Berkeley, CA 94704 USA
www.northatlanticbooks.com

Printed in the United States of America

You Are More Than Your Body: 30+ Evidence-Based Strategies for Living Well with Chronic Illness is sponsored and published by North Atlantic Books, an educational nonprofit based in the unceded Ohlone land Huichin (Berkeley, CA) that collaborates with partners to develop cross-cultural perspectives; nurture holistic views of art, science, the humanities, and healing; and seed personal and global transformation by publishing work on the relationship of body, spirit, and nature.

North Atlantic Books's publications are distributed to the US trade and internationally by Penguin Random House Publisher Services. For further information, visit our website at www .northatlanticbooks.com.

ISBN 979-8-88984-237-8 (pbk.) — ISBN 979-8-88984-238-5 (ebook)

Library of Congress Cataloging-in-Publication data is available from the publisher upon request.

The following information is intended for general information purposes only. Consult with your own therapist or clinician to find a mental health plan that works for you. Any application of the material set forth in the following pages is at the reader's discretion and is their sole responsibility.

The authorized representative in the EU for product safety and compliance is Eucomply OÜ, Pärnu mnt 139b-14, 11317 Tallinn, Estonia, hello@eucompliancepartner.com, +33757690241.

1 2 3 4 5 6 7 8 9 KPC 30 29 28 27 26 25

For anyone who has ever felt different. And for Sean. Thank you for being my person and choosing me every day. You're my favorite.

Contents

Author's Note

Dear Reader,

Thank you for taking the time to pick up this book. It is something I have thought about writing for quite some time with the hope that my experiences as a disabled woman, along with my professional knowledge and expertise as a clinical psychologist, will be of value to others. My intention is that as you read this book, there is something in it that resonates with you and is helpful to you. If this book enhances the well-being and quality of life of a single reader, I will be very thankful.

With gratitude,
Jen Caspari

Introduction

OUR LIFE EXPERIENCES CAN greatly influence what we think, feel, and do. They can lead to a sense of understanding, behavior change, and personal growth. Often, growth follows some sort of distress or personal challenge. If everything in your life is going smoothly, and you have no concerns or difficulties, there is likely no stimulus for insight or change. I have played the mental game with myself of wondering what my personality might be like if I was not born with a physical disability. Would it be greatly different? Would I have the same level of grit, determination, stubbornness, and empathy? There is no way to know the answers to these questions, yet I am confident that living with a disability has strengthened the resolve I feel to live life in a way that is meaningful to me and the empathy I have for others. And these are traits that I value. Does this mean my life is better because I have a disability? Not necessarily. It simply means my disability has created current circumstances and challenges that have enhanced valuable attributes of my personality.

While I am not opposed to positive thinking, and believe our thoughts can have a big influence on our mood, emotions, and behaviors, I am not an advocate of the "Just think positively" school of thought or the belief that "There must be a silver lining to this difficult situation." Often, it is not authentic or realistic to "think positively," and it is more helpful to acknowledge the complexity of our experiences, which is why I typically focus on practicing neutral or balanced thinking (more on this later). Distress and growth tend to go hand in hand, as do pain and joy. What we do matters, and there is power in practicing effective coping skills and engaging in values-based actions. For example, we can improve our quality of life if we align our daily behavior with our personal values and what is meaningful to us.

That is why it was important to me to write this book and outline several helpful coping skills, based on my personal and professional experience, that I believe can facilitate determination, courage, self-acceptance, and quality of life. Life is hard and complex. To live well we often need to practice embracing vulnerability, taking emotional risks, and prioritizing what is meaningful to us. The more we practice tuning in to our internal experience, and the more knowledge we have of helpful skills that enhance cognitive, emotional, and behavioral flexibility—not holding too rigidly to one way of thinking, feeling, or behaving, the ability to take on different perspectives, consider different choices, and so on—the more options we have and the stronger our well-being, quality of life, and the possibility of a life well lived.

The phrase *coping skills* is used frequently throughout this book. It is common to think of coping skills as the methods a person uses to manage stressful situations. Within this book, I broadly define coping skills as the tools and techniques used to support or enhance overall mood, well-being, and quality of life. Also, I refer to certain thoughts and behaviors as unhelpful. I intentionally use the label of unhelpful to imply that thoughts and behaviors may be unhelpful in the moment, worsening mood or well-being or moving us away from our values, while not being unilaterally unhelpful. Further, labeling something as unhelpful is more neutral than labeling it as bad, and using neutral language allows us to separate our thoughts and behaviors from our core sense of identity and to be less judgmental toward ourselves.[1] Having an unhelpful thought or engaging in an unhelpful behavior does not mean you are a "bad" person.

In the following chapters, you will find a variety of coping skills presented in a brief, and hopefully easily digestible, way. The book is divided into three sections: managing your emotions, balancing your thoughts, and caring for your body. I discuss aspects of my personal experience living with a disability that relate to the skills presented, provide self-reflection exercises to aid self-awareness, and offer information based on my knowledge and experience as a clinical psychologist on what the skills are and how to go about practicing them. I recommend reading the book with a journal or notebook nearby so you can practice the self-reflection exercises as you go.

While the skills I offer are general and relate to overall mood and well-being, I use the lens of my experience of living with a disability as a framework to discuss the skills, and I wrote this book with those who struggle with low self-esteem, self-worth, or self-acceptance in mind. You don't have to be living with a disability, chronic health condition, or overt difference to benefit from the skills as they are broadly helpful tools. Nonetheless, my personal experience may resonate more deeply with you if you have a disability or chronic health condition.

As you go through this book, I offer the encouragement to slow down and pause as needed. It may be helpful to read the skills more than once and circle back to them over time. Feel free to take what resonates with you and leave what does not. Also, remember that learning any type of new skill, and developing the ability to implement it effectively, requires practice, patience, and repetition. Be compassionate with yourself. Pretty much everything in this book falls under the category of "Easier said than done." And, when in doubt, repeat, repeat, repeat.

Finally, learning to ground yourself in the present moment and calm your body and nervous system is a beneficial skill set that supports the implementation of other coping skills. Whether chronic pain or fatigue is increasing, or perhaps you are feeling more irritable, anxious, or unsettled, grounding and relaxing your body are important ways to slow down, take care of yourself, and set yourself up to have more ability to utilize additional coping skills as needed.

Some of what you read in this book may provoke certain emotions in you and feel emotionally challenging. That is why I want to offer a couple of supportive skills at the end of this section that you can start practicing now. Additional body-based coping skills are discussed in part 3 of the book.

Why Am I Writing This Book?

I was born almost three months prematurely, weighing about two and a half pounds, and have cerebral palsy (CP). CP is a group of disorders that affect movement and muscle tone. It is caused by damage to the immature, developing brain, often before or during birth. The cause of CP and its effect on function vary.[2] My early birth was sudden and unexpected as my mom had a healthy pregnancy to that point with no indications for the possibility of a premature birth and had two full-term pregnancies before mine. My mom likes to say that I just couldn't wait to be born and that I came into the world smiling, as I have always been a very smiley person. The severity of my CP is mild, and I walk with a limp. My muscles are tight and spastic, and I mostly have problems with my legs and feet. I also have poor balance, and my lower spine curves, causing back pain. My tight muscles constantly work and compensate for my unbalanced and limping gait, leaving me sore and tired. I have had several orthopedic surgeries throughout my life, and I have had to learn, following some mild emotional breakdowns in shoe departments as a teenager, that my feet will never be "normal," and I just can't wear certain types of shoes.

My parents gave me every opportunity they could, and without the great resources they provided, I would likely be in a different physical place today. They evaluated and addressed each issue I had. Did I need more physical therapy (PT)? What about another orthopedic surgery? Am I walking better with or without my orthotics? I started PT around the age of two and participated consistently until age thirteen, at which point I declared I was done with PT.

While I was scared of surgery as a child, and not a huge fan of seeing orthopedists or doing PT, in retrospect, these experiences contributed to my grit and determination. They taught me to have agency over my actions and move toward what is important to me. They highlighted that some aspects of my life are unchangeable and out of my control and that I can also choose to go after what I want.

I entered college wanting to be the next Katie Couric. I was a broadcast journalism major and dreamed of conducting captivating interviews and being on TV. As I participated in reporting classes, it became clear to me that the seemingly typical lifestyle of a reporter was not for me. I didn't like the idea of chasing down sources or not having set work hours. I am someone who likes consistency and routine. Yet, what was clear to me was my interest in people. I liked learning about human behavior and people's life experiences, and I wanted to help others. My psychology classes were interesting and enjoyable and it was a natural decision to focus on psychology instead of journalism. I was committed to learning how to help others improve their daily lives, and after a terminal master's degree in community counseling, I decided to earn a doctorate in counseling psychology to further my knowledge and expertise.

Living with a disability influenced my professional interest in health psychology and my understanding of the psychological aspects of health and wellness. I have worked in a variety of settings, including hospitals and medical clinics, and much of my career as a clinical psychologist has focused on helping people with acute and chronic health conditions improve their daily functioning and quality of life. I have also concentrated on managing mood concerns such as anxiety and depression and guiding people in taking values-based action that facilitates a sense of meaning and purpose.

I wrote this book because I believe my knowledge and skills as a clinical psychologist along with my lived experience as a disabled woman can benefit others. I have spent the past twenty-five years learning and practicing psychology, and have cultivated my interest in and empathy toward others for even longer. I hope my experiences provide a sense of human connection and allow you to feel seen and understood.

My clinical work aims to empower my clients to live the life they want to live, a life that feels meaningful. It is normal to feel stuck or to feel like you are simply existing. Yet, it is possible to get unstuck and take realistic and doable action to improve well-being and quality of life even when challenges and difficulties exist. This book is aimed at giving you the tools to do just that.

Two Helpful Skills to Use Now

5-4-3-2-1 Grounding Technique

Grounding skills are skills that use the senses to calm and ground you in the present moment when you are feeling emotionally overwhelmed, caught in your thoughts, or generally disconnected from the present moment. When you notice yourself feeling overwhelmed or disconnected from the moment, practice pausing, taking a couple of slow breaths, and then going through the below steps to ground yourself.

5—Name five things you can *see* around you. This can be anything in your environment that you see.

4—Name four things that you can *touch* around you. This may be the chair or couch you are sitting on, the ground beneath your feet, a piece of clothing, and so on.

3—Name three things that you can *hear.* This can be any external sound you hear. Maybe you hear an air conditioner, a car or bird outside, or music playing.

2—Name two things that you can *smell.* Maybe you can smell scented lotion or a candle. If you can't smell anything in the moment, feel free to walk nearby to find a scent, or you can name two things you like the smell of.

1—Name one thing you can *taste.* Are there any tastes in your mouth like gum, coffee, or food you recently ate? If not, you can name one thing you like the taste of.

It can also be helpful to end the exercise by naming one thing you like about yourself.

Lengthen Your Exhale Breathing Exercise

The exhale part of the breath is like the brake in a car: It slows your nervous system down. One type of relaxation breathing is to intentionally lengthen your exhale. If, for example, you naturally inhale to about a count of 3, you would practice exhaling slowly to a count of 5 or 6. In general, it is helpful to make the exhale about twice as long as the inhale.

To practice this type of breathing, I encourage you to stop what you are doing a few times a day, or whenever needed, and for a couple of minutes take slow breaths focusing on lengthening your exhale. It may be helpful to count to yourself as you inhale and exhale. So, slowly counting 1, 2, 3 as you inhale, and then slowly counting 1, 2, 3,

4, 5, 6 as you exhale. If you get distracted, gently return your attention to your breathing. Aim to practice for about two to five minutes. If you are feeling a moderate to high level of distress, practicing this exercise for longer, about ten minutes, will be beneficial.

This can be a great exercise to practice when pain, stress, or anxiety, for example, are increasing, yet you don't have to wait to practice! The more you practice breathing exercises when you are feeling generally calm, the more likely you will remember to use them when distress increases, and the more effective they will be.

Part 1

MANAGING
YOUR
EMOTIONS

CHAPTER ONE

Learn Emotion Regulation Skills

YOU ARE PROBABLY FAMILIAR with the 0 to 10 pain scale: On a scale of 0 to 10, with 0 being the least and 10 being the most, how bad is your pain? On most days, my pain and fatigue levels sit at about a 5 out of 10.

Feeling chronically fatigued and experiencing chronic pain can lead me to feel irritated and be emotionally reactive. Or, I may seem irritated, yet I am simply tired. A common refrain between my partner and me is him asking me, "Are you angry?" and me replying, "No, I'm not angry. I'm tired." Of course, I can feel both tired and angry. Angry that I'm so consistently tired or in pain. Angry that I rarely experience physical ease and comfort. Even if I am not initially irritated or angry, it can be challenging for me to feel fatigued and act calmly and patiently. For example, I can feel irritated when I am fatigued and there are tasks to do like going to the grocery store or cleaning. Even small tasks like unpacking my lunch bag at the end of the workday can fuel irritability because I just don't want to do anything in the moment other than sit and rest. My irritability will then lead me to be impatient and talk to my partner in an angry tone of voice. Also, I am prone to wanting to complete tasks as soon as possible, so I may feel irritated or stressed that there are any tasks to do. But that does not necessarily mean I need to do them right away. I may just think I do, and that expectation creates a sense of pressure or urgency that increases irritability and fatigue.

Emotional regulation is the ability to manage and effectively respond to emotions or the ability to have control over our emotional state. Usually, this involves using skills that decrease the intensity or duration of emotions.[1] For example, when I am feeling irritated, emotional regulation would involve acknowledging my irritability and then taking a few slow breaths to lessen irritability. Research suggests that emotional regulation is related to mood and depression, work efficiency, relationship satisfaction, and perception of well-being.[2]

We often use a wide range of skills to regulate our emotions. For example, you may try to distract yourself from certain emotions or aspects of a situation that are fueling your emotions, practice thinking about a situation in a more balanced or neutral way to lessen the intensity of your emotions, practice making room for your emotions, or try to suppress them or push them away. Some emotional regulation skills are more adaptive than others. For example, suppressing emotions typically leads to more emotional intensity over time.[3]

The intensity of emotion is a key component of emotional experience that influences motivation and behavior. For example, intense levels of anxiety can lead to feeling overwhelmed, frozen, and unable to act. Research suggests that more intense negative emotions require people to use a higher number of regulation skills.[4] Emotional regulation can be more challenging when living with a chronic health condition or disability. For example, if you are experiencing a migraine and are in physical pain, you may feel stronger negative emotions and have more difficulty helpfully regulating emotions based on the combination of physical discomfort and negative emotions. Or, if someone makes a derogatory comment about your disability, you may feel self-conscious and embarrassed, which fuels self-criticism and leads you to think about the situation in an overly negative way, which in turn hinders your ability to effectively regulate your emotions.

My irritability tends to be the worst at the end of the workday as I have used up the gas in my internal tank and am more fatigued. Fatigue is another aspect of living with a chronic health condition or disability that makes emotional regulation challenging.[5] Often my irritability will peak as I am getting home from work or when I am washing up for bed. It is as if my body is telling me that I have passed a point of no return on the fatigue dial. Knowing this about myself, I will regulate my emotions by intentionally saying soothing and compassionate statements to myself when I get home from work or while washing up for bed, such as "You are tired. It's okay. You'll be resting soon." Or, "You worked hard today. I'm proud of you. The working part of the day is done." If I need an added dose of self-soothing, I pause, take a breath, and put a hand on my chest as I say these statements to myself, which soothes me and helps ground me in my body and the present moment.

Emotional Reactivity

Emotional reactivity refers to the frequency and intensity of emotional arousal. It includes the threshold and ease with which someone becomes emotionally aroused and the intensity of emotional experiences.[6] For example, someone who becomes irritable very quickly and easily, and experiences a high level of irritability, may be emotionally reactive.

I encourage you to take some time to think about these questions about emotional reactivity and write out your responses in your journal.

- Do you tend to feel emotions strongly? If yes, do you feel certain emotions more strongly than others?

- On a scale of 0 to 10, with 10 being extreme, what is an average emotional intensity level for you?

- Do you tend to get upset, frustrated, or disappointed easily?

- Do your emotions typically linger for a long time, or do they move through you quickly?

- What tends to trigger strong emotions in you? Are there common or frequent triggers?

- How do you typically react or behave when experiencing strong emotions?

◆ Has the intensity of your emotions, or how you respond to them, caused any difficulties in your life? For example, in your relationships?

◆ How would you like to respond when feeling strong emotions? Is there a more helpful way of responding compared to what you typically do?

Tuning In to Internal Experience

Before you practice regulating your emotions, you need to know how you are feeling in the moment and how intense your emotions are. You can practice tuning in to your moment-to-moment internal experience by pausing (defined as briefly stopping what you are doing) for a minute or two as you go about your day and noticing and naming your internal experience by asking yourself the questions below. Noticing and naming your experience help to bring nonjudgmental attention to it,[7] and it is important to name your experience without judgment or criticism. For example, you are not judging your experience as good or bad. You are practicing observing and simply naming it.

◆ What **thoughts** are going through my mind? Practice noticing any specific thoughts you are having by completing the sentence, "I am having the thought that . . ."

◆ What **feelings** are here? Practice noticing and naming whatever feelings are present in the moment. For example, anxiety, anger, sadness, frustration, joy, happiness, excitement, boredom, and so on. Then, rate how intense the emotions feel on a scale of 0 to 10, with 0 being not intense at all, and 10 being extremely intense.

Keep in mind that it can be difficult to differentiate between thoughts and feelings. Thoughts are ideas in our minds. They can be about ourselves, others, and the world around us. Thoughts include beliefs, opinions, and assumptions and are the words or images that are in our minds as we go about the day. Feelings are responses or reactions we feel inside us. They are our subjective emotional experiences.

At times, simply the process of naming emotions can reduce their intensity. It may be helpful to name the emotion silently to yourself, say it out loud, or write it down. It is also useful to use a feeling list as a reference when noticing and naming your feelings as a list of different emotion words may help you reflect on your experience in a more nuanced way, versus automatically defaulting to certain emotion words that you are familiar with yet may not fully capture your experience. I have included a Feelings List below, and you can go online and search for "feelings list" for additional examples. Also keep in mind that it is common to feel multiple feelings at once, including feelings that may seem contradictory.

- ◆ What **physical sensations** are here right now? How does my body feel in this moment? Do I feel physical tightness, soreness, heaviness, or something else?

Feelings List

calm	courageous	confused	incapable
centered	brave	empty	resigned
capable	indifferent	trapped	content
fulfilled	confident	resistant	vulnerable
patient	daring	shut down	stressed
peaceful	determined	uneasy	tense
relaxed	grounded	withdrawn	burned out
serene	proud	embarrassed	cranky
joyful	accepting	ashamed	depleted
amazed	connected	shame	exhausted
delighted	compassionate	guilty	edgy
eager	caring	humiliated	frazzled
ecstatic	affectionate	mortified	overwhelmed
energized	loving	self-conscious	rattled
engaged	concerned	useless	restless
enthusiastic	empathy	worthless	shaken

excited	safe	timid	unsettled
happy	curious	afraid	fearful
inspired	interested	anxious	dissatisfied
invigorated	fascinated	apprehensive	reluctant
lively	intrigued	frightened	shocked
passionate	stimulated	hesitant	unsettled
refreshed	sad	nervous	ungrounded
rejuvenated	despair	panic	suspicious
renewed	anguish	scared	unsure
satisfied	depressed	terrified	thrilled
despondent	worried	angry	disappointed
helpless	annoyed	discouraged	grateful
agitated	heartbroken	appreciative	aggravated
hopeless	delighted	disturbed	lonely
fortunate	exasperated	unhappy	humbled
frustrated	teary	regretful	furious
weary	remorseful	grouchy	yearning
sorry	hostile	disconnected	hopeful
impatient	lethargic	encouraged	irritated
listless	optimistic	irate	removed
expectant	outraged	numb	powerful
resentful	bored	powerless	upset
PHYSICAL SENSATIONS			
achy	frozen	trembly	shivery
burning	heavy	sore	hollow
buzzy	jumpy	clammy	knotted
clenched	light	cold	loose

tight	nauseous	stiff	numb
hot	pounding	constricted	prickly
dizzy	pulsing	dull	radiating
electric	rigid	empty	tingling
fluttery	shaky	wobbly	warm
sweaty	drained	vibrating	breathless

Adapted from the book *Nonviolent Communication* and the Hoffman Institute Foundation's "Feelings List."[8]

Emotion Intensity Scale

0	1	2	3	4	5	6	7	8	9	10
not intense			moderate intensity					extreme intensity		

Meeting Basic Needs

It is challenging to practice helpful coping skills that enable us to be less emotionally reactive if basic physiological needs, such as thirst, hunger, needing sleep, or being hot or cold, are not met. For example, when I am thirsty, my irritability increases, and it becomes difficult for me to focus on things other than my thirst. Truly, thirst and dehydration are frequent triggers for irritability and feeling unwell overall. It may sound simple, and a helpful thing I can do for myself when feeling short-tempered is to drink some water.

This relates back to Abraham Maslow's theory of human motivation.[9] Maslow suggested that human beings have a hierarchy of needs (physiological, safety, love and belonging, esteem, and self-actualization) and we are instinctively motivated to meet our basic needs first. This may be true; however, someone may not have access to enough food throughout the day, or be unable to keep full due to a condition like Crohn's disease. In these types of situations, I would suggest doing the best you can and remember that you may not be able to meet all of your basic needs, yet you may be able to meet some of them. For example, perhaps it is difficult to keep your stomach full, and you do your best to drink water or dress in layers of clothing so you can help keep yourself at a comfortable body temperature.

Once basic needs are met, we can aim to meet higher-level needs. Despite this, we often ignore our basic needs as we go about our day, striving to complete an ongoing list of tasks. So, it is important to practice tuning in to your body and overall physiological needs throughout the day so you can meet unmet needs, as possible, and set yourself up for having an increased ability to practice additional coping skills. Further, research suggests that interoceptive awareness, the conscious awareness of bodily sensations, is linked to overall emotional awareness and regulation.[10] Keep in mind, however, that there are many reasons why it might be difficult to tune in to your body—for example, if you have experienced disordered eating, a traumatic event, or have chronic pain. More specifically, if you have a history of ignoring cues of hunger and fullness, it may be challenging to tune in to these physical cues. Or, when someone has experienced persistent stress or trauma, it is common for them to either feel disconnected from their body, often as a form of self-protection from distress, or hyperarousal, which is a heightened state of physical anxiety.[11] Or, you may automatically have the urge to ignore or distract yourself from physical sensations if you are experiencing chronic pain because you don't want to feel the discomfort of pain.

If it feels challenging to connect to your body, aim to be gentle with yourself and notice your basic needs as you can. Or, start by tuning in to physiological sensations that feel safer and less overwhelming. For example, maybe it feels a bit easier to notice that you feel thirsty rather than trying to notice how your whole body feels.

One way you can identify if you have unmet physical needs is to practice identifying and naming body sensations. You can use the physical sensation words in the Feelings List above as a reference, or you can touch a certain area of your body—your shoulder, for example—and then describe the sensations you feel. You can also enhance your ability to bring your attention to your body by taking a few slow breaths and noticing the sensation of the air flowing in and out of your body (your chest or belly rising and falling) or intentionally tense an area of your body and then release the muscles, noticing the difference in sensation when the muscles are tense versus relaxed. For example, make a tight fist, hold it tightly closed for a few seconds, and then open and relax your hand muscles.

A few times per day, pause and ask yourself, "How is my body feeling right now? Am I thirsty, hungry, hot, cold?" If the answer to any of these questions is yes, take action to meet the need. Drink a glass of water, have a snack, take off a layer of clothing, or put on a layer. Relatedly, it can be helpful to plan to meet your basic needs. If leaving the house, pack a water bottle and snacks. Take an extra layer of clothing. Here is a brief list of ways you can meet your basic needs that in turn will aid you in practicing the other coping skills throughout this book.

Drink water: You don't necessarily need to drink water nonstop to be hydrated. Yet hydration is significant to our overall body function and mood, and it is important not to ignore thirst.[12] Dehydration can increase stress, make it more difficult to focus, and make it more difficult to have a bowel movement. I am thirsty when I wake up in the morning, and one strategy I use to aid hydration is starting my day with one or two glasses of water right when I wake up.

Eat regularly: Part of tuning in to your body is noticing your cues for hunger and not ignoring them. Eating regularly helps support a stable level of blood sugar, which helps support your mood.[13] I'm guessing you have heard of being hangry: irritability because of hunger. If feeling cranky or irritable, you may want to pause, check in with your body, and see if you are hungry.

Regulate temperature: As possible, aim to regulate your body temperature. It can be difficult to focus on other needs or tasks if you are freezing cold or burning up. A simple tip: Dress in layers that you can remove or add as needed.

Rest and sleep: It is easy to have a go-go-go mentality and ignore your need for rest and sleep. Give yourself permission to rest and sleep. You are not a machine. Your body has limits. Resting and sleeping are essential to your well-being and allow you to engage in activity in a more effective and meaningful manner.

Move your body: My pain, soreness, and stiffness increase if I am sitting for hours on end or standing still for a while, and it can be helpful to change physical positions. If possible—not everyone has the privilege of mobility—shift positions, move around, or stretch. For example, if you have been sitting for a while, do some shoulder rolls or stand up and walk around the room for a minute. You don't have to go for a thirty-minute walk to move your body. Also, it can just feel good to move. Movement can be joyful. Dance party in the kitchen, anyone?

Shifting Mental Focus

Shifting mental focus can be difficult. It is easy to focus on how fatigued I am, how sore and achy my muscles are, and how, at times, it's difficult to pay attention because I am so tired that my brain just shuts off. It's easy, yet unhelpful, to constantly focus on these things. One thing that helps shift my attention is thinking about what I am grateful for. Dwelling on distressing thoughts, particularly when thoughts are related to a reality we cannot change, is tiring and zaps energy, and I don't need to be zapping energy!

I want to be clear that it is natural and normal to feel anxious, sad, angry, and demoralized, and focusing on gratitude is not meant to serve as a way for me to minimize or avoid uncomfortable emotions. I allow myself to feel sad, mad, whatever it may be. Allowing and accepting our complete emotional experience, including emotions that may feel negative or unpleasant, are key components of psychological flexibility and well-being. It is normal to think of certain emotions as bad or negative, yet they are simply messengers that inform us of our needs.[14] Just because an emotion may feel unfamiliar or uncomfortable does not mean it is bad or harmful.

Acceptance and commitment therapy (ACT) proposes that psychological problems result from psychological inflexibility and engaging in rigid and unhelpful thoughts and behaviors aimed at avoiding unpleasant or unwanted experiences. Cultivating psychological flexibility involves being present, allowing your full experience, being aware of your values, and engaging in values-based behaviors.[15]

Acceptance of emotional experience also involves practicing opening up to and making room for unpleasant or unwanted thoughts, feelings, and sensations and not fighting with or pushing away your internal experiences.[16] It is helpful to practice naming and acknowledging your experience, allowing it to be there, and letting it come and go at its own pace. One way you can practice this is by practicing mindfulness and tuning in to your experience nonjudgmentally in the present moment. See chapter 5 for more information on mindfulness.

Since it is easy for me to dwell on whatever feels unpleasant, and start to feel stuck, after a certain amount of time I tend to say to myself, "Jen, how do you want to be spending your mental and physical energy right now?" And I remember that I have a choice over where I put my attention and energy. It is hard to feel content about life when I am complaining all the time. So, I strive to focus my energy on things I can control or am grateful for, not as a way to push away unpleasant experiences but as a way to facilitate taking steps to engage in activities that are meaningful to me, regardless of coping with fatigue and pain.

Below are some tips for shifting mental focus:

Pause. I don't mean to be a broken record, and to practice additional skills you first have to practice pausing and noticing what is happening in the moment. Are you ruminating or dwelling on a certain thought? Does your brain feel stuck on a certain thought almost as if the thought is stuck on a piece of sticky Velcro in your mind? Or is your mind a broken record where the same thought is repeated instead of moving on to the next verse in the song?

Focus on something mindless. Aim to give your mind a break. Play a mindless game on the computer, watch a video, color, or fold laundry. Engage in an activity that doesn't require mental effort.

Or intentionally focus on something that takes mental effort in a different way than focusing on an unhelpful thought. Play a challenging game. Read a thought-provoking book. The aim here is to occupy your mental energy with an engaging and pleasant task.

Switch scenery. It can be helpful to your mind to get a change of scenery, and sometimes all that is needed is to simply move to a different room. Or, if possible, go for a walk outside. Physical movement and fresh air are often invigorating and can enhance a sense of mental clarity. If going outside isn't a good option, engage in movement inside. If you are physically able, stretch, do a few push-ups, do yoga or Pilates exercises, or use available exercise equipment.

Breathe. Take several slow breaths. Practice lengthening the exhale portion of the breath. The exhale is like putting on the brakes in a car; it helps slow down the nervous system. For example, if you naturally inhale to a count of 3, aim to exhale to a count of 6. Or try breathing only using your nose. You may naturally breathe more slowly when breathing from your nose versus your mouth, which can be relaxing.

Power of the Pause

If you can't already tell, I am a fan of pausing, of taking a moment or two to stop. Pausing is a skill that you can intentionally practice throughout the day. One reason I love pausing is that it helps us practice other useful skills. To practice skills or change your behavior, you must first practice being aware of your internal experience and then slow down enough in the moment to give yourself the option of doing something different. Shifting out of autopilot, or acting without awareness, is one of the primary functions of pausing.[17] Pausing enables awareness of the present moment and engagement in intentional behavior, including how you respond to stress, and sets the stage for creating options and change. Pausing can also be beneficial on its own. It has been associated with decreased negative reactions to unpleasant events,[18] more effective learning, and problem-solving.[19] Further, pausing is a way to give yourself a mini-break or reset, to remind yourself that life does not have to be one long obstacle course where you race from one challenging task to the next. You have the power to choose your behavior, and pausing is often a helpful place to start.

Challenges come along with having cerebral palsy: chronic fatigue, which is at times all-consuming and can cause my brain to "shut off," irritation related to fatigue, chronic pain, and rarely experiencing the feeling of physical fluidity or ease—I can become tearful when I imagine the ease of fluidly walking up or down a set of stairs, easily taking one's shoes off while standing, comfortably squatting and picking something off the floor, or effortlessly getting up from a sitting position. I personally and professionally believe in the helpfulness of practicing pausing to effectively cope with challenging situations—the ability to stop and notice your experience in the moment—and then make an intentional decision about a helpful way to act versus reacting automatically in a way that may not be helpful: learning to respond versus react. Responding implies an element of thoughtfulness, of slowing down long enough to ask yourself, "What am I experiencing right now, and what would be helpful to me in this moment?"

Cultivating the ability to pause when you are feeling pretty darn good is one thing. Pausing when emotional or physical sensations intensify is another. When my fatigue increases, it is much more difficult for me to pause and act with intention. I know intellectually it will be beneficial for me, and those around me, to act with less irritability, for example, and I still find myself becoming irritable and reactive, even if not in an extreme way. I speak with a more irritated tone of voice, I have less patience, I feel more easily bothered, or the actions of my partner feel more personal. During these times, it is helpful to remind myself that pausing and intentionally acting more compassionately and patiently will save me energy and create more ease and calm internally and in my environment.

This is not to say that I ignore my emotions and physical sensations. It is important that I deliberately acknowledge my fatigue and irritation and shift my behavior. Maybe this means intentionally slowing down and being self-compassionate when I feel the urge to criticize myself about not getting to bed as early as I wanted and rushing to put my head on the pillow (I consistently want to go to bed earlier in an attempt to ease the never-ending fatigue). Maybe this means saying a kind word to my partner when moments before I was criticizing him in my head, or it would simply be helpful to take a couple of slow, deep breaths. Pausing also helps us recognize and remember that we don't necessarily need to do anything more. Often, a beneficial action is stopping and allowing ourselves to be, as we are, in the moment. Whatever form it takes in the moment, learning to pause has been crucial in managing my fatigue and pain, calming my nervous system, and regulating my emotions.

CHAPTER TWO

Cultivate Unconditional Self-Compassion, Self-Acceptance, and Self-Worth

USUALLY, IN MY MIND, I am not disabled. If I am walking in a dream, I don't limp. When I am walking, in general, I'm not tuned in to my limp. I am just walking, unless circumstances pull my attention to CP: My fatigue or muscle soreness increases; my legs are particularly stiff; my right foot knocks into my left leg, causing me to slightly stumble; there is snow or ice on the ground, or any situation that requires a level of balance I don't have, such as stairs without a railing or a mound of something on the sidewalk that I need to step over. Because I am not often tuned in to my limp, I can be caught off guard when someone asks me about it. *Oh, yeah, right,* I think, then reply in the manner of, "Yes, I limp. I was born prematurely . . ." In certain situations, I have been really startled. A disheveled stranger coming up to me in a drugstore asking what is wrong with me. "Nothing, thanks. I'm fine," I reply as I turn and walk in the other direction.

Don't get me wrong; I think about my disability every day, and when I do, I am usually complaining to myself. "I am so tired, sore, tight!" "I really need to stretch!" I am thinking about unpleasant physical sensations, and I feel these sensations, yet I am disconnected from the more complete felt experience of my body. I spend a lot of time thinking about my body, yet I am not necessarily in my body, connected and attuned to sensations and the feeling of my body as a whole. Embodiment is a sensory experience where we feel our body and have a sense of wholeness, where the body and mind are connected rather than separate or distinct.[1] I view embodiment through a mindfulness lens that involves being tuned in to the sensations of the body, and connected to the felt sense of the body in the present moment, instead of thinking about the body.

One of the ways I was disconnected from my body when I was younger was by focusing on thoughts that I was unattractive. Whenever I saw myself walk, either on a video, in a mirror, or in the reflective glass of a building, it was upsetting because I thought I was ugly and worried others would think the same thing. I avoided seeing myself walk, which in turn made my inaccurate thoughts about my disability and my distress stronger. If I happened to walk past a reflective surface, I would stare straight ahead or down at the ground. I would not watch videos of myself where I was walking because seeing the images was emotionally jarring and made me feel unattractive, unworthy, and isolated. I worried that my different body would be judged as inferior and unacceptable by others and that I would not have the same fun and exciting experiences as my able-bodied friends.

I knew I was avoiding seeing myself walk because I thought I was ugly and inferior, and I didn't want to face that. With time, I also knew that by not facing my limp I was making these thoughts, and my low self-worth, more powerful. The thoughts were strong. I did think I was ugly. And a small part of me knew that was not true. If I didn't directly face my limp, I would never learn to accept myself or challenge my inaccurate and unhelpful beliefs that my limp was unattractive and made me inferior to able-bodied people. These were thoughts, not facts. While I could practice challenging these thoughts without seeing myself walk, learning that my thoughts were untrue, and that I have worth and beauty as I am, would be stronger and more resonant if I directly exposed myself to my limp. So I slowly started to not look away if I saw myself walking, and sat with whatever thoughts and feelings came up. If I thought I was ugly, I acknowledged the thought and reminded myself that my thoughts were not the truth. Over time, when I walked down the street and saw my reflection in a building, or saw a video of myself, I told myself, "Really look at yourself. That is you. That is how you walk. That is okay. It's not ugly or bad; it's a limp."

I needed to learn to acknowledge my disability and work to accept it. Knowing it is permanent; knowing it is something that makes me different, but not less than. Realizing that I was using valuable energy by criticizing it or avoiding it. I needed to practice viewing my body and disability neutrally and with less self-criticism. Body neutrality includes cultivating a neutral attitude toward the body that is realistic, mindful, and flexible. It involves appreciating the broad functionality of the body and recognizing that self-worth is not based on appearance.[2] Research suggests that developing body neutrality facilitates appreciation for the functionality of the body, body satisfaction, positive mood, and less appearance-based comparison to others.[3] You don't have to completely love your body, or yourself, to cultivate self-compassion and self-acceptance and increase body satisfaction.

Body Neutrality

Below are tips for cultivating body neutrality.

Respect your body. Aim to respect your body by caring for it (meet your basic needs as possible, rest, give yourself physical comfort, and so on) and think about it matter-of-factly and non-judgmentally using an "It is what it is" mentality. Strive to respect your body whether you feel positive, negative, or neutral about it.

Take the middle ground. It is common to think in an all-or-nothing manner. You may tell yourself that you either love your body or hate it. Yet, thinking this way can fuel distress and criticism. Aim to think about your body in a neutral, middle-ground way. For example, maybe you don't like the shape of your face but you like your eyebrows. Acknowledge what you like or appreciate about your body.

It's okay not to love your body. You don't have to love your body to respect and appreciate what it does for you, and you don't have to put pressure on yourself to love it if that is not how you feel. Again, aim for neutrality, not love.

Focus on function. Body neutrality focuses on the function of the body, and being appreciative of what it can do (digest food, breathe, etc.) rather than focusing on appearance and what the body looks like. Next time you notice thinking about what your body looks like, practice shifting focus to what your body can do.

Self-worth is not based on appearance. Acknowledge and celebrate intrinsic traits you value about yourself that are not based on appearance (your unique personality, qualities, values, etc.). And acknowledge and grow helpful external factors of self-esteem such as engaging in enjoyable hobbies and friendships.

Body image is flexible. Remember that body image is flexible and changes. How you feel about your body today may not be how you feel about it tomorrow. Practice holding your thoughts about your body lightly and flexibly, and give yourself room to change and grow depending on your values and what feels helpful to you at the time.

With time, I practiced accepting myself as a whole person, including my disability, and realized that I am worthy in my entirety. While self-acceptance is an ongoing process that can be easier said than done, it was only when I learned to accept myself as I am that I was able to have more confidence and trust in myself and not, on some level, think my disability is something that makes me inferior or something that I have to apologize for.

Self-Acceptance

I encourage you to take some time to think about these questions about self-acceptance and write out your responses in your journal.

+ What thoughts do you have about yourself? Thoughts may be related to your personality, appearance, or behaviors.

+ Are there parts of yourself that you tell yourself are bad, ugly, inferior, or not good enough in some way? If so, what parts, and what do you tell yourself?

+ Have you had these thoughts for a long time or are they new?

- Does it feel like these thoughts are permanent and unchangeable? What is an alternative perspective? What would a loved one say to you about your thoughts?

- What do you appreciate about yourself? For example, do you appreciate certain personality or character traits, passions, hobbies? Perhaps you appreciate that you are loyal, funny, trustworthy, caring, or curious.

- What are your strengths?

- What do your loved ones appreciate about you, or what would they say about you?

- What do you admire in others? Which of these characteristics do you have?

Self-acceptance is a person's acceptance of all facets of themselves. It involves the recognition that you are human, unique, complex, and imperfect, and can include believing in your capabilities and body acceptance.[4] Unconditional self-acceptance is self-acceptance without conditions, meaning it is not based on meeting certain standards or requirements. You can be aware of your limitations and areas of growth, yet this awareness does not hinder your acceptance of yourself. This may sound straightforward, yet most of us have learned to regard ourselves as conditionally acceptable—I am acceptable if I am well-coordinated enough, well-spoken enough, strong enough. We tend to blame ourselves or view ourselves as inadequate in some way. To enhance self-acceptance, it is helpful to explore the parts of yourself that you have difficulty accepting. And if you can decrease self-judgment and self-criticism, you can foster acceptance. Self-criticism and self-acceptance are two sides of the same coin, and cultivating self-acceptance requires more self-compassion.

To become more self-accepting, it is helpful to ask yourself specifically what it is you don't accept about yourself and bring compassion and understanding to all parts of yourself. Also, self-acceptance is different from self-improvement. Self-acceptance isn't about fixing anything about yourself; it is about affirming who you are in all aspects. Self-acceptance has a here-and-now focus. It is about practicing being okay with who you are today without qualifications. This does not mean you ignore things that you may want to change (assuming these things are under your control and you can change them). It means these changes are not necessary to feel self-acceptance—you accept yourself regardless. Changing behavior is a matter of personal choice, not a requirement for acceptance. Overall, the aim is to accept yourself as you are today, right now—to give yourself unconditional approval. You do not have to earn acceptance. You can choose to accept yourself right here, right now in all your imperfections, in all your humanness.

Self-acceptance leads me to think about comparison and how it can fuel self-criticism. It is important not to keep up with the Joneses. It is natural to compare ourselves to others and to get caught in a mental comparison loop, and this is rarely beneficial. You may have heard the phrase "Comparison is the thief of joy." It is difficult to compare yourself to others and feel joy at the same time. If you are using comparison to broaden your perspective and enhance your sense of gratitude it can be helpful, yet this is not a common form of comparison. Typically, comparison leads to feeling inadequate or inferior in some way. "I am not as successful, competent, attractive as they are. Why don't I have what they have?" We use comparison as an avenue for self-criticism: "What's wrong with me? I must be inadequate," which hinders self-acceptance. I compare myself to others all the time, yet I also know that I feel most content when I support and encourage those around me and focus on what is important to me, not how I stack up against others. For example, if I am speaking to another professional who appears extremely competent and well-accomplished, I may tell myself that I am not as skilled or successful as I could be and that I need to do more. Or, if a friend is taking fun vacations every few months, and I haven't been on a vacation in a long time, I may think my life is boring and uninteresting. These comparisons fuel distress and pull my focus away from my values and priorities. Also, they reinforce the thought that I am not good enough as is, which is untrue.

Relatedly, we typically speak to ourselves much more harshly and critically than we speak to others, and we treat others with more compassion than we offer ourselves. Again, self-criticism erodes self-acceptance. How can I foster self-acceptance if I am constantly criticizing myself? One way you can decrease self-criticism and enhance self-acceptance is by practicing self-compassion. You can do this by talking to yourself in a caring and kind tone of voice and offering yourself words of comfort, understanding, grace, and affection.

Self-Compassion

Dr. Kristin Neff, a researcher and pioneer in self-compassion, defines self-compassion as being open to your struggles, having feelings of caring and kindness toward yourself, treating yourself with a non-judgmental attitude about perceived inadequacies, and recognizing that your experience is part of being human.[5] Research suggests that self-compassionate people experience fewer negative emotions, ruminate less about mistakes and negative events, and more effectively cope with negative events. Further, self-compassionate people tend to think about themselves more accurately, and how they perceive themselves is less dependent on achieving certain outcomes.[6] A key component of developing self-compassion is recognizing when you are being self-critical and practicing talking to yourself with kindness and understanding.[7]

Cultivating Self-Compassion

If it feels unnatural or difficult to talk to yourself compassionately, it can be helpful to think about a person or animal that you care deeply about and consider how you would talk to them, particularly if they were going through something challenging.[8]

1. Bring to mind a person or animal you care about. This could be someone in your life or a person you know of, real or fictional, that you respect and admire. Think about them going through a difficult situation. Perhaps they are feeling distressed, uncertain, overwhelmed, or struggling to treat themselves kindly. What would you say to them?

2. Think about specific caring and encouraging statements you would say to them. It may be helpful to write down examples in your journal. For example, "This sounds really difficult, and it also sounds like you are doing the best you can." Or, "I am here for you. I know you will get through this even if it is tough." Or, "You are a capable person and it will be okay."

3. Now, practice similarly talking to yourself. Aim to talk to yourself in a noncritical, calm, and comforting way.

It can be beneficial to practice repeating self-compassionate statements to yourself, particularly whenever you notice yourself being self-critical or harsh (which will likely be often). These statements can feel unfamiliar and awkward at first because our self-critical voice tends to be well-ingrained and automatic. However, with practice, these statements sound more authentic and comforting. Below are examples of self-compassion coping statements. Feel free to use any that resonate with you or create your own.

Self-Compassion Statements: Talking to Yourself as You Would a Loved One

- This is a moment of difficulty.
- I am not alone. Other people feel this way too.
- This moment will not last forever.
- I am okay.
- I am perfectly imperfect.
- I am human.
- I am capable.
- I believe in myself.
- I can be kind to myself.
- I can practice accepting myself as I am.
- I can give myself compassion.
- I can practice caring for myself.

Practicing Gratitude

I have so much in my life that I am grateful for. I have been fortunate to live a life filled with privilege, good fortune, and opportunity, and I think it is important to acknowledge the privilege I have, particularly when so many do not. For example, I grew up with love and support from my family, had sufficient financial resources, and was given educational opportunities that allowed me to easily pursue higher education and graduate study. Yet, when my pain and fatigue intensify, it is all too easy to focus on the unpleasant physical sensations and to forget, or gloss over, my deep sense of gratitude. Practicing gratitude enables us to have a more balanced outlook. Research has demonstrated that negative information is given more mental weight in our minds than positive information,[9] and gratitude helps us notice and appreciate the positive aspects of life.[10] It is important not to use gratitude to minimize or push away your concerns and challenges. For example, it is possible to feel drained, distressed, and grateful at the same time.

Gratitude is similar to appreciation. It is an expression of appreciation, or thankfulness, for what we have in life, big and small. Dr. Robert Emmons, psychology professor and gratitude researcher at the University of California, Davis, has explained that gratitude includes two components: affirmation of the good things we have received in life and acknowledgment of the role other people have played in the good fortune in our lives.[11] Therefore, it can be helpful to both internally acknowledge the things we are grateful for and outwardly express thanks to others who help and support us. Gratitude is a skill that you can practice and strengthen over time, and by cultivating a stronger sense of gratitude, you may feel more joy, less stress in your daily life, and a greater sense of self-esteem. Fostering gratitude often begins with observing, or noticing, moments of gratitude in daily life. Saying "Thank you" to someone, or having an internal feeling of joy or excitement, for example, can be signals of gratitude, that you are appreciative of someone or something. See if you can practice briefly pausing when you have the instinct to say

"Thanks," or feel a sense of joy, and see if you can name what you are grateful for in the moment.

Research suggests that people with physical disabilities can feel hopeless and uncertain about their future. They may worry about their place in society, being able to obtain and maintain a job, or being rejected by others, among other things. Overall, those with disabilities can feel pessimistic about the future.[12] Optimism is the cognitive tendency to expect and predict positive outcomes and have a sense of hope that positive events will occur. Optimistic individuals tend to feel confident, have better health outcomes, for example, fewer incidences of cardiac disease and stronger immune response, and pursue desired goals.[13] Gratitude and self-esteem have been found to be linked with optimism, and research suggests a relationship between practicing gratitude, self-esteem, and optimism in people with disabilities. People with disabilities who practice gratitude pay attention to positive aspects of life, have hope for the future, and feel more self-esteem and confidence in their accomplishments.[14]

One way I practice gratitude is by noting one thing I am grateful for each morning as I start my day. I have observed that I often note fairly small things, such as the enjoyable taste of my morning cup of coffee or the feeling of the sun on my face. Other times, I note gratitude for larger aspects of my life, such as my relationships.

Below are some additional ways you can practice gratitude.

Keep a gratitude journal. Like my daily practice above, establish a daily practice in which you remind yourself of the things you are grateful for. You can set up this practice however you like. Perhaps you start your day by verbally stating one thing you are grateful for, like I do, or end your day by writing down three things you are grateful for that day.

Remember what you have accomplished and how far you have come. It can be beneficial to spend some time thinking about challenges you have overcome or are continuing to cope with, and things you have accomplished in life, particularly when doing so was not easy. By recalling challenges, you also can recall things you have been grateful for along the way and now.

Think about your relationships. Intentionally bring to mind a person you care about and ask yourself, "What have I received from, or am I receiving from, this person?" The answer to this question can highlight aspects of your relationships that you are grateful for.

Share your gratitude. Don't keep your gratitude to yourself! The next time you feel a sense of gratitude for a family member, friend, or colleague, let them know. Chances are doing so will feel pleasant to you and to them, and expressing gratitude to those around you can strengthen your relationships.

Tap in to your senses. The human body is a complex and miraculous thing. By intentionally tuning in to your senses—the ability to see, hear, taste, touch, and smell—you can remind yourself of all the amazing things the body can do.

Visual reminders are your friend. Forgetfulness and lack of mindful awareness can be two barriers to practicing gratitude. So, it can be helpful to use visual reminders that encourage practice. I use a daily reminder that pops up on my phone at the same time each day. Or you can use a sticky note that you place somewhere you will see each day—on the bathroom mirror or on the inside of the door to your home.

Make a commitment. At times, making a written commitment to practice a skill can help enable practice. It may be helpful to write a gratitude commitment, "I commit to practicing gratitude each day," and post it somewhere you can see.

Use gratitude language. Intentionally practice regularly using words that evoke a sense of gratitude, such as *grateful, appreciative, fortunate, thankful, glad,* and so on.

Take grateful action. Engage in small daily actions that help foster gratitude, such as smiling, saying "Thanks," and sending others gratitude texts or letters.

Here's a gratitude list you can create in your journal, which you can use daily or weekly, to jump-start your gratitude practice.

My Gratitude List

- ◆ Something good that happened today (or this week) is . . .
- ◆ I'm grateful for my loved ones because . . .
- ◆ I'm grateful for my friendship with _____ because . . .
- ◆ I'm grateful for who I am because . . .
- ◆ Something small I am grateful for is . . .
- ◆ An act of kindness I received or witnessed is . . .
- ◆ A joyful experience I had is . . .
- ◆ Something else I am grateful for is . . .

When I am stuck in a "My body hurts—I'm so tired—this is terrible" mindset, it is not easy to feel gratitude or be self-compassionate. The more physically depleted and stressed I am, the more I struggle with my pain and fatigue, focus on what I believe is going wrong, and am more self-critical. It is easier to feel self-acceptance and solid self-worth when feeling good. The challenge is unconditional self-acceptance and self-worth.

Unconditional self-acceptance has been associated with psychological well-being and lower levels of anxiety and depression.[15] It is distinct from your abilities, accomplishments, and the perception of others. Unconditional self-acceptance is not about what you have done or are doing. It is not about comparison to others, being well-liked, or proving yourself through performance. Of course, it is natural and not problematic to want to be liked and well thought of by others, particularly people you respect and care about. Research suggests that being likable signals to others that you are accommodating and helpful, and being popular may signal your ability to accomplish tasks. Both likeability and popularity can enhance a person's sense of social confidence and well-being.[16]

We don't live in a vacuum, and social support and relationships, including having relationships in our lives that feel supportive and reciprocal, contribute to self-esteem and well-being. For example, a lack of responsiveness in relationships can decrease relationship quality and increase distress.[17] Further, it is instinctive to try to confirm our sense of competency and worth through the acceptance and approval of others.[18]

Nonetheless, unconditional self-acceptance entails fully valuing yourself regardless of your performance or if others approve of you.[19] Unconditional self-acceptance facilitates unconditional self-worth, and the belief that you are worthy and have value as a person as is— the belief that you are inherently a valuable and perfectly imperfect person.

Tips for Fostering Unconditional Self-Worth

Practice forgiveness. If you notice yourself struggling with past actions, behaviors, or perceived mistakes, intentionally practice forgiving yourself. Reflect on the factors that led to past behaviors (you may be automatically zooming in on certain factors and ignoring others, or perhaps not acknowledging the complexity of the situation. Remember, hindsight is twenty–twenty), acknowledge your emotions, and identify what you learned from the situation. Then say to yourself, "You are human. I forgive you," in a compassionate and genuine way.

Use your imagination. Practice noticing thoughts you have about how you should be different and letting these thoughts come and go without giving them deliberate focus or attention. One way you can do this is by using imagery. For example, imagine your mind as the sky and your thoughts as clouds or birds that move in the sky, or your mind as a stream and your thoughts as leaves floating down the stream, or your mind as a conveyor belt and your thoughts as boxes or luggage that you place on the conveyor belt. You can learn more about using imagery to create mental distance from your thoughts in chapter 4.

Practice appreciation. Instead of focusing on how you should be different, intentionally bring to mind something you appreciate or value about yourself or even something you feel neutral about.

Through this practice, you are acknowledging you are worthy as you are.

Be there for yourself. The next time you experience a feeling of sadness, rejection, loneliness, isolation, or embarrassment, practice acknowledging how you are feeling and offering yourself some comfort and compassion. Place a hand on your chest and say to yourself something along the lines of, "I am hurting in this moment. I'm not alone. Others hurt too."

Emotional Vulnerability

Broadly defined, to be vulnerable is to be susceptible to being hurt or wounded or to having your interests threatened.[20] Humans are vulnerable to physical harm such as illness and injury as well as emotional harm. Some researchers have defined vulnerability as facing a significant chance of being harmed while lacking the ability or means to protect oneself.[21] I encourage you to take some time to think about the following questions about emotional vulnerability and write out your responses in your journal.

- What is something you want to do but haven't done?
- Why haven't you done it? Do your thoughts and feelings play a part—for example, feeling anxious or assuming a bad outcome?
- How would you feel if you didn't act?
- What types of situations make you feel anxious, scared, or worried?
- Have you settled for less than you want or desire? If so, why?
- If you only had a few more months to live, what would you regret not doing?
- What are your core values? (See "Values" in chapter 6 for guidance.) Are you living by them?
- Describe a time you felt nervous or scared about doing something and still did it.
- When do you feel proud of yourself?

Relationships are a fundamental part of being human. Our lives involve interacting with other people and our relationships can provide us with care, support, and love. Relationships and social interactions also potentially bring criticism and rejection. Emotional vulnerability is the feeling of being exposed to possible emotional attack, harm, criticism, or rejection. And while criticism and rejection can come from others, they can also come from ourselves. For example, being vulnerable may mean going after a meaningful goal that has an uncertain outcome, and knowing that if you do not achieve the outcome you want, you may criticize yourself.

It is not easy to take emotional risks and open ourselves up to the possibility of being hurt. Yet, like distress and growth going hand in hand, vulnerability and growth go hand in hand. By having the courage to be vulnerable and open ourselves up to meaningful experiences, we learn and grow. Researchers have suggested that courage combined with vulnerability is a strength and personal resource, and being vulnerable is a way to embrace being authentic and human. Further, emotional vulnerability involves the courage to feel and express a full range of emotions and therefore facilitates interpersonal connection and the sense of being cared for and understood by others.[22]

Embracing vulnerability is a skill that you can practice. On the first day of the year-long clinical internship program that I completed as part of my doctoral degree, I was handed a training binder. The first page of the binder was blank except for two words: *Embrace Vulnerability*. This struck me. The takeaway for me was that I would likely learn all sorts of clinical skills over the year, and the most valuable skill I could learn was to embrace vulnerability. One concrete way I practiced this throughout the year was directly and confidently saying "I don't know" when asked a question I did not know the answer to and not pretending I knew or apologizing for not knowing. Instead of saying, "I don't know; I'm so sorry," I said, "I don't know, and I can do my best to find the answer."

Humans have a strong instinct for self-protection, to avoid pain and hurt. However, being vulnerable is part of being human. Being vulnerable requires us to let our guards down and be seen for who we authentically are. This is difficult, and a key part of enhancing acceptance, developing genuine confidence, and building connections and deep relationships is allowing ourselves to be fully seen by ourselves and others.

Vulnerability is an inevitable part of life. So many things require vulnerability: trying something new, sharing a challenging experience, saying "I love you." If you constantly have a guard up, you often end up living a less fulfilling life. Instead of trying to guard against it, you can practice embracing vulnerability, knowing that it is helping you move toward what is meaningful to you.

There are many benefits of practicing embracing vulnerability and taking emotional risks. As mentioned above, practicing vulnerability increases a sense of courage and resiliency. Emotional vulnerability and the expression of genuine feelings and desires cultivate authenticity instead of focusing on pleasing others or avoiding rejection. Relatedly, sharing your full range of feelings helps create understanding, builds empathy, and fosters stronger connections and relationships. Before you can express your emotions, you have to be aware of them, so being vulnerable can also enhance personal insight. Research participants reported that being vulnerable and taking risks led to feeling more confident, capable, and having a greater sense of personal agency while also making life more interesting and exciting.[23]

Here are some strategies for how to practice embracing vulnerability:

Give yourself permission to be yourself. Remind yourself that we are all human and we are all imperfect. Repeat helpful statements to yourself that facilitate permission-giving: "I am human." "No one is perfect." "I am allowed to be myself." "I don't have to apologize for who I am." "I am a perfectly imperfect and complex person."

Practice being guided by your values, not worry or anxiety. Remind yourself of what you value and what is meaningful to you in life. In other words, what is the "why" behind your behavior?

Learn about yourself. What are your preferences, needs, opinions, and desires? What matters most to you? When do you feel most energized? When do you feel drained? Thinking about and knowing the answers to these types of questions allow you to have stronger self-awareness and to make informed decisions that help you move forward even when you're feeling uncertain or insecure. If you don't know yourself well, you may be prone to acting based on a sense of should versus your personal values.

Be nonjudgmental and curious about all your emotions. Instead of using a critical or judgmental tone of voice with yourself—"Why am I anxious again? What is wrong with me? I shouldn't feel this way!"—practice using a curious and matter-of-fact tone: "Huh, I notice I'm feeling anxious right now." If you are having trouble identifying your feelings, it may be helpful to use a feelings list to guide you; see the Feelings List in chapter 1.

Try new things. This can be challenging, and it is okay to start small. What is something you have wanted to do or try yet haven't due to feeling uneasy or uncertain? See if you can act on something important to you even if you feel anxious. Developing courage is not about feeling calm and confident. It is about feeling anxious and taking action anyway. Ask yourself, "Can I have the courage to practice showing up to myself and my life and allow myself to be seen by others?"

Be less concerned about what other people think. It is normal to be worried about the perception of others. Yet, this worry can hinder helpful behavior, and we almost always assume others are going to be more concerned about us and more critical of us than they are. We tend to be much more critical of ourselves than other people are. To help practice being less concerned about what others think of you, notice and name your automatic thoughts and create more helpful, and balanced, thoughts that you can repeat to yourself whenever your automatic thoughts pop up (see the "Common Unhelpful Thinking Habits" handout in chapter 4). Also, you can ask yourself, "What would I do right now if I wasn't worried about what others think?" and focus on practicing that behavior.

Practice self-compassion. To embrace vulnerability, it is helpful to practice being kind and compassionate toward yourself and recognize your humanness. One way to practice self-compassion is by saying or repeating self-compassionate statements to yourself. See the "Self-Compassion Statements" listed earlier in this chapter for examples.

CHAPTER THREE

Practice Radical Acceptance

WHEN I WAS YOUNGER, I was not very comfortable around other people with disabilities because I was not comfortable with myself. I grew up in an able-bodied world, and I did not routinely spend time with people with disabilities. I never really associated myself with the disabled world and did not fully acknowledge or accept my disability. Not fully recognizing or integrating my disability into my self-concept created a psychological disconnect in my life and hindered my self-acceptance and self-worth.

It was clear throughout my childhood that I could not do certain activities that my siblings or friends participated in. When my siblings went to a sports camp in the summer, I hung out with my mom. Yet, my parents had the general mindset that I could do almost anything others could do, and they sought to remove whatever barriers they could. I felt their support and encouragement, and it was emotionally painful to be different and lack certain physical abilities. While I understood my physical differences intellectually from a very young age, it has taken me much longer to emotionally accept the reality of my disability.

During my elementary school years, I took tap and jazz dance classes and gymnastics with friends. I enjoyed these activities and, for the most part, I don't recall thinking much about my disability or talking about how I couldn't dance or tumble like the other kids. I took gymnastics one evening a week for about two years with the main goal of being able to do a handstand, which I thought was a great feat. I never reached my goal, and, for me, the gymnastics classes consisted of stretching, jumping in a foam pit, and attempting a partial handstand using a wedge against the wall while the other kids in the class did a variety of tumbling. I didn't talk about not reaching my goal and what it meant to me not to be able to dance or tumble like the others; I just went to class.

It is difficult to feel different, or "other," especially during the formative childhood and teenage years. Overall, I was lucky growing up. My peers were kind to me and I was rarely teased or made fun of. However, certain memories stick with me, as I am sure is true for everyone, like having to run outside in gym class in third grade, and after the whole class was done and standing in a line on the side of the grass watching and waiting, the only runners who remained were me and a kind girl with Down syndrome. The boys in the class were pointing and laughing at us, and I remember feeling so embarrassed and wishing I could be with the rest of the class. Or, around fifth grade when we took a big field trip to a museum a couple of hours away and my friends did not want me to be a part of their assigned group due to concern that I would slow them down and they wouldn't get to see as much of the museum. Or, the rare occasion growing up when a mean-spirited person would laugh at me and imitate my limp, leading me to feel ashamed and embarrassed—that visceral sensation of anxiety, my face becoming flushed and my heart beating faster as I was being called out for my difference, my inferiority, my lacking.

Feeling judged by others is hurtful, and this can be especially true if we are judged about an aspect of ourselves that we have no control over—physical mobility, race, sexuality, etc. What am I supposed to do if someone is judging me about my disability? There is nothing I can change (assuming I even think there is something that needs changing). The message that is sent is that my being is wrong. How I am as a person is unacceptable. It is easy to internalize this message and try to ignore or deny the seemingly inferior parts of ourselves.

In retrospect, I realized that I did not talk about feeling sad about being different or other psychological aspects of my disability much growing up, and as a result, I did not acknowledge the sadness or sense of loss that I felt. As an adult, I asked my mom, who has strong psychological awareness, why it seemed like my emotional reactions to my disability and being different from others were not really talked about. She replied that I always seemed happy and overall there were no indications that I was feeling upset or that it would be helpful for me to emotionally process my disability more directly. She is right. I was happy; I am happy. I am also a person who for a long time did not fully acknowledge my disability and how it impacted me.

I didn't want to be different. To have parts of my body that were misshapen and, to me, ugly and embarrassing. To limp, have limitations, and be unable to do many physical activities that were easy for others. Can I do a lot of things? Yes. And there is a lot I can't do. I can't take a kickboxing class, go for a run, or stand on one foot, at least not well. I can't walk up or down stairs without a railing or do any type of activity that requires a decent amount of balance. I can't wear high-heeled shoes (or lots of types of shoes). Many of these things may seem superficial or inconsequential, and they are still losses that we can grieve.

Grief is a reaction to loss and can include feelings of sorrow, emotional numbness, or anger. Living with a chronic health condition or disability can create losses in life that include loss of mobility, role changes, inability to engage in certain activities, loss of control, financial stress, relationship challenges, changes to future plans and goals, and changes to self-identity or perceived sense of health. The chronic nature of certain health conditions can also create recurring loss and serve as a continual reminder of loss, which in turn can cause a sense of continual sorrow.[1] Also, uncertainty is a common aspect of chronic health conditions as physical symptoms, and the overall impact of the condition on daily life, may fluctuate, making it hard to predict how you will feel one day to the next and what activities will be doable. It is also common to worry about the condition worsening and experiencing more challenges and loss over time,[2] and to feel uncertain due to a loss of control.

Living with uncertainty, and more specifically intolerance of uncertainty, has been associated with anxiety, grief, distress, and a decrease in self-compassion.[3] Uncertainty is often experienced as uncomfortable and stressful, and while it is natural to feel intolerant toward uncertainty, because intolerance is associated with distress, it is important to practice managing and tolerating uncertainty. Below are some tips for doing so.

Acknowledge uncertainty. Denying or trying to suppress uncertainty can intensify it. Practice matter-of-factly and nonjudgmentally naming uncertainty. For example, "Not knowing how I am going to feel day-to-day is hard. I wish I could predict how things will go."

Create realistic expectations. Expecting predictability, or believing you can control things that you can't, can increase disappointment and distress when things are unpredictable or outside of your control. So, create realistic expectations and remind yourself that aspects of your life are beyond your control.

Talk with others. Talking with others about uncertainty and how it is challenging to manage can feel validating and supportive and make it easier to navigate.

Remind yourself of your ability to cope. Uncertainty can feel intolerable because it feels threatening, and you may worry that you won't be able to cope if your condition worsens or there is a highly stressful event. Remind yourself that even if things do not go smoothly, you are a capable and resilient person and can cope.

Uncertain does not equal bad. While it is true that positive outcomes cannot be guaranteed, it is also true that negative outcomes are not guaranteed. We often automatically think that uncertainty will lead to a bad outcome because it feels dangerous, and we want to protect ourselves from a bad outcome. Yet, uncertain simply means unknown. It does not automatically mean bad, and the chance for a bad outcome is not necessarily higher than a positive or neutral outcome. So, it can be helpful to say to yourself, "Unknown does not equal bad."

Come back to the present moment. Uncertainty is about the future. More specifically, it is focused on the fear of the unknown in the future. Mindfulness is a helpful antidote to future-oriented worry as it involves nonjudgmentally connecting to the present moment. One way you can practice mindfulness is to intentionally pay attention to the physical sensations of your breath as you breathe in and out (the sensation of the air in your nose or your chest and belly rising and falling). If your mind wanders to thinking about the future, gently bring your attention back to your breath. Mindfulness is discussed in more detail in chapter 5.

Emotional processing is an important part of grieving that can facilitate acceptance of the reality of loss, uncertainty, and change. Acceptance of loss does not mean emotional pain goes away, rather it involves not resisting what already exists, understanding what loss means for your life currently, and moving toward values-based goals. Emotional processing entails developing awareness of your emotions, allowing and feeling your emotions, and exploration and reflection to increase understanding of your emotional experience.[4]

Self-Reflection Exercise: Loss and Acceptance

I encourage you to take some time to think about these questions about loss and acceptance and write out your responses in your journal.

- ◆ What losses have you experienced?

- ◆ What about yourself, or your circumstances, do you have a hard time accepting? This may include loss and uncertainty.

- ◆ Think about these things and sit with them for a few minutes. What thoughts, feelings, or physical sensations arise?

- ◆ Why are these things difficult to accept? For example, do they evoke unpleasant thoughts or feelings? Do they bring up a sense of disappointment, loss, or missing out on something?

- ◆ Does not accepting yourself or your circumstances create difficulties for you? If so, what are they?

- ◆ Similarly, would being more accepting be helpful to you? If so, how? For example, would it possibly create a sense of internal ease or enable helpful behavior such as taking action toward a meaningful goal?

◆ What parts of yourself or your life do you value or provide you with a sense of meaning and purpose?

Radical Acceptance

Dr. Marsha Linehan, the renowned psychologist and creator of dialectical behavior therapy (DBT), defines radical acceptance as "letting go of the illusion of control and a willingness to notice and accept things as they are right now, without judging." It is a "complete and total openness to the facts of reality as they are, without throwing a tantrum and growing angry."[5]

It can feel like a tall order to radically accept a situation that we don't like and that feels unpleasant. I have been living with a disability for over forty years and I continue to find myself wishing aspects of my disability were different. Often this wish comes from a place of emotional or physical difficulty. I'm tired. My body hurts. It feels like a slog to get through the day.

At the same time, I am my body. By that, I do not mean that my physical body encompasses all that I am as a person. I mean that my body cannot be separated from the rest of me, and by fighting my body I am fighting myself. Pain is the feeling of unpleasant physical sensations or emotions. Suffering is separate from pain and often involves a struggle with, or denial of, pain. It consists of an interpretation of pain based on a person's thoughts, beliefs, and judgments. Suffering is related to distress that arises when a person thinks their sense of self, sense of control, or view of the future is threatened. It can also be related to a lack of meaning or feeling powerless in the face of pain.[6] Suffering is associated with a person's attitude, the resources they have available to them to manage and cope with their experiences, and the choices they make.[7] This is where the phrase "Pain is inevitable, suffering is optional" comes from. You can experience a lot of suffering, and increase the sensation of pain, when you fight against what is, particularly when you fight against things that are beyond your control.

It is natural to feel upset, to seek comfort and ease, to want distress or unpleasant sensations to go away, to have things be different, be better. This is a dialogue that can run in my mind repeatedly. If only I wasn't disabled. If only I didn't have fatigue, pain, muscle spasticity. Sometimes, I try to imagine what life would be like if I didn't have CP. In many ways, the idea of having less physical discomfort sounds wonderful, and it is also difficult to fully imagine as CP influences my daily experience. One of the benefits of having a disability or chronic health condition is that you are forced to realize, in often a more direct and visceral way, that there are things in life you cannot control.

This does not mean I am always skilled at placing my attention on things I can control, but I know that it is futile to spend my mental and physical energy caught in a tug-of-war with my disability or anything outside my control, including the behavior of others, especially when my energy is limited to begin with. Pain in life is a given, yet I do agree with the notion that suffering is often optional. Suffering can manifest in thoughts or behaviors that fuel the fire or pour salt on a wound. I may be fatigued and in physical pain. I may feel sad that I don't know what it feels like to move with effortlessness, yet I don't have to suffer. And we can suffer in small ways. Suffering with a lowercase *s:* the little, and seemingly insignificant, ways I increase my distress. I may be fatigued, yet if I spend energy fighting with the fatigue, I am creating suffering. Instead, it is helpful to mentally step back, acknowledge the reality of my experience and circumstances in any given moment, and ask myself, "How do I want to use my energy right now?" or, "What would be helpful?" or, "How can I be my authentic self within the reality of this moment?"

Radical acceptance goes hand in hand with the idea of living with ease. Living with ease does not mean the absence of difficulty or challenge. Like radical acceptance, I think of living with ease as not struggling with the reality of the current moment, not fueling the fire of distress, and focusing on being present. We all experience stress in daily life, and it is important to be aware of the ways we amplify our stress so we can limit doing so. I know I don't need to feel more stressed and drained. This does not mean I tune out or ignore stress or other challenges. Rather, I choose to not get into a tug-of-war with it. Living with ease also often entails slowing down, aiming to calm your nervous system if you are feeling overly activated, practicing gratitude, and reminding yourself what you are thankful for. Again, the goal is not to minimize your distress, but to broaden your perspective and help yourself more fully tune in to the moment in all its complexity. You can simultaneously be stressed and be connected to the present moment and thankful for the supportive people around you, for example.

A common misunderstanding I hear from clients is thinking acceptance is the same as resignation, giving up, or approval of circumstances that you genuinely don't like. Accepting reality does not mean you are resigned to or approve of the current circumstances. It simply means you fully acknowledge what is happening in the moment. Interestingly, research has shown that acceptance facilitates change because you are letting go of struggling with ineffective behaviors.[8] You are no longer doing what isn't working, and often what isn't working is wanting so badly for things to be different that you do the same unhelpful behaviors repeatedly. Sometimes the struggle to change blocks change.

Acceptance also does not mean you are passively resigned to societal problems such as discrimination and oppression. For example, research has shown that experiencing more frequent racial discrimination was associated with more severe mental health symptoms, and how a person responds to discrimination can play a role in the level of distress they experience. More specifically, using active coping skills, such as seeking out social support and taking action against discrimination, is associated with lower mental health symptoms and can buffer against the relationship between discrimination and mental health symptoms.[9]

Embracing reality helps free up energy as you are not using energy fighting against reality, and it helps create options and engagement in active, beneficial, and values-based behaviors. I am a believer in the power of options. It is human nature to view the world, and our own thoughts and behavior, through a rigid all-or-nothing lens. This can be limiting. We often automatically assume there is only one way to think about or do things. This is rarely the case.

Developing and enhancing your ability to think about different options are essential components of developing cognitive and behavioral flexibility. There is power in *or*, in knowing there are options and possibilities. I could spend my time and energy resisting my fatigue in this moment. Or I could spend a few minutes taking slow breaths. Or I could watch a relaxing TV show. Or I could text a friend. Or I could take a walk outside. The world is already a limiting place, and not everyone has the same external options as everyone else. Perhaps, then, it is all the more important to practice radically accepting things as they are in the moment, understanding what is in your control, and recognizing you have options for how you relate to your internal experience and the behaviors you engage in.

Here is a summary list of why it is helpful to practice radical acceptance:[10]

- Acceptance decreases emotional distress.
- Acceptance increases willingness to have one's experiences.
- Acceptance facilitates and expands helpful behaviors.
- Acceptance enhances compassion.
- Acceptance can create a sense of ease.

Developing Radical Acceptance

1. First, think of an event or situation that you have a hard time accepting. It could be currently happening to you or something that has happened in the past that you catch yourself ruminating over. If you start to feel too overwhelmed when thinking about a particular event, it might be helpful to start with a less overwhelming yet still important event or situation.

2. What caused the event? Try to think of all the facts that led to the event or situation you have a hard time accepting and write them down. Try not to judge yourself or place blame when you write down the causes of the event. State the facts. Don't judge something as good or bad. This is not meant to undermine the pain you've been through or are currently experiencing. You

are practicing nonjudgmentally naming the facts and finding a way to move forward.

3. Accept the feelings: Practice nonjudgmentally observing whether certain emotions arise in you when you are thinking about this event or situation. Perhaps you feel frustration, anger, or sadness. Be open and try to observe any physical sensations in your body as a manifestation of emotions. It might be an obvious sensation or something milder, such as mild muscle tension in your shoulders, chest, or stomach. Whatever you feel, see if you can practice making room for it and allowing it to be present. You don't have to like it. Simply practice allowing the emotions and physical sensations to be there and nonjudgmentally observe them (name them without judging them as bad: "I feel a weight on my chest" or "I feel anxious and my stomach muscles are tight"). Remind yourself what you can and cannot change. Over time, you may feel an increased sense of ease by practicing accepting your emotions and physical sensations.

4. Make a plan: The last step is making a proactive plan about the situation or its effects. If it is something that doesn't affect you in a significant way, then it might be enough to just practice radical acceptance (the previous steps) and gradually come to terms with the situation. Or, if it does affect you in an unhelpful way, try to think of how you can realistically improve the situation. Of course, this could take many forms depending on the situation. Examples may be to practice having realistic expectations, not making assumptions about other people or situations, practicing direct communication, and so on.

Another way to practice radical acceptance when you are experiencing thoughts, emotions, physical sensations, or a situation you are having a difficult time accepting is by using coping statements. These statements are meant to remind you that there are some things you cannot change. By accepting reality as it is, you can decrease judgmental thoughts, tension, and distress.

Radical Acceptance Coping Statements

Below are examples of radical acceptance coping statements. Pick the ones that seem the most helpful to you and keep them somewhere you can easily access whenever needed, for example, on your phone. If you think of other coping statements you like, don't hesitate to create your own.

- The present moment is the only one I have control over.
- Fighting my thoughts, emotions, or physical sensations only gives them more fuel to intensify and grow.
- The present is the result of dozens of past variables.
- This moment is what it is even though I might not like it.
- I cannot change what has already happened.
- I accept this moment as it is.
- Although my emotions or physical sensations are unpleasant, they will not last forever.
- Although my emotions or physical sensations are uncomfortable, I do not have to struggle with them or push them away.
- Although this moment is unpleasant, I can cope with it as it is.
- It's not helpful for me to fight the past.

Part 2

BALANCING YOUR THOUGHTS

CHAPTER FOUR

Change Your Relationship with Your Thoughts

I TRIP AND FALL on a fairly regular basis. Usually, I fall when I am not paying attention to the uneven ground below me; when I walk, I am constantly having to look down so I can assess the ground and how I need to move to limit falling. Or I am tired and dragging my feet, leaving me more vulnerable to catching a piece of a sidewalk. No matter how many times I've fallen before, falling jars me physically and emotionally, physically because one moment I am upright and the next I am on the ground, and emotionally because it throws my disability to the front and center of my mind, which can lead to various reactions. When I fall, I may feel disbelief: "Did I really just fall again? This is getting ridiculous"; somewhat guilty: "I may truly hurt myself one day. I need to be more careful"; annoyed: "I am tired of falling. I wish I didn't need to pay such close attention to my walking"; embarrassed: "Did anyone see me? That must have looked so clumsy." So falling isn't just about falling, it's about me continuing to accept being disabled and genuinely believing that my disability does not make me inferior. Once, after tripping over a towel on the floor and falling, I said to my partner, "Sorry you have to be with the girl who is always falling." What I was actually saying is, "Sorry you have to be with a disabled person. I feel bad for you and myself." I know this isn't an empowered way to think, but those thoughts sometimes rise to the surface, which is natural.

One day during college, while walking around campus, I fell three times in one day. Let's just say I was extremely embarrassed. And the seemingly worst thing someone did for me in that situation was to come up and say, "Are you okay? Here, let me help you." Inside I wanted to shout, "Please don't bring more attention to me! Thank you and go away." I just mumbled something like, "I'm okay, thanks." In other words, "There is nothing to see here!" I didn't want to feel like there was a spotlight on me, and falling made it feel like my disability was even more visible and noticeable. Yes, I was limping before I fell, and now I was on the ground making it even more obvious that I am different. And in this context, different felt bad. It felt inferior, embarrassing, and unattractive.

I'm guessing no one really likes falling in public, yet the varying intensity of my embarrassment after falling was interesting. My level of embarrassment and distress was related to my body image and level of disability acceptance. Broadly defined, body image is the feelings and attitudes one has toward their body.[1] The more accepting I was and the more neutral or positive my feelings and thoughts about my body, the less embarrassed and distressed I felt. In more recent years, I am less bothered when I fall because I am more accepting of my disability and difference. I recognize falling is not a personal flaw or inadequacy. It is just something that happens. More importantly, I know that my disability is not a defect, something to feel ashamed or embarrassed of, or something to try to hide or separate myself from.

Shame and embarrassment come from the belief that something is wrong or bad. For example, society stigmatizes disability by associating being disabled with being undesirable and unworthy and viewing disability as a negative and all-pervading attribute that covers all other personal attributes and skills. When people with disabilities live in an environment where they are devalued and seen as unattractive, they come to see themselves as unattractive and devalue themselves. Further, stigma leads to disconnection and being cut off and othered by society, and this sense of being othered may lead people with disabilities to feel ashamed. There are also societal norms and ideals related to attractiveness and the ideal body, including strength, independence, and physical fitness, which are constantly promoted and affirmed in the media. Therefore, people with disabilities may feel shame, embarrassment, and a negative body image due to thinking they are not measuring up to the societal ideal.[2]

My disability, my body, is not shameful. It is not an inappropriate behavior I need to change. I am not inferior or lacking because my body moves differently than most bodies. Nonetheless, my initial emotion when falling may be embarrassment or shame. My thoughts in the moment have a big influence on my emotions. If I fall and say to myself, "This is so embarrassing! People are going to think I am clumsy and weak," I am going to feel embarrassed and anxious. If I tell myself, "Yes, you feel embarrassed right now, and that's okay. It isn't the end of the world. People fall. It doesn't mean anything negative about you," or if I remind myself, "Your disability is not a defect that needs to be changed," I feel calmer and more self-assured. So, changing our thoughts to be more balanced and helpful has a beneficial impact on our emotions and behaviors.

When we think that we are flawed, and feel insecure, we often assume our perceived flaws stand out to others as if illuminated by a spotlight, which leads to self-consciousness, embarrassment, or shame. We are fearful of being judged, criticized, or rejected by others while judging and criticizing ourselves. This fear is based on the belief that we are lacking and inadequate, which can relate to any insecurity, including insecurity about our bodies and physical appearance. For example, research on shame in those with chronic illness has found that living with a chronic illness involves loss of independence, alterations in self-image, changes in social roles, and changes in the ability to do certain tasks, which can lead to negative self-evaluations, self-blame, and feelings of shame.[3] Further, it is normal to want to present a positive version of oneself to others to protect against possible criticism and judgment, and people with chronic illness may talk about their condition in a way that fits accepted societal norms. For example, if society associates illness with weakness, and people do not want to be perceived as lazy, weak, constantly complaining, or attention-seeking, they may only mention positive aspects of their experience, downplay challenges, or not talk about their illness experience.[4]

Your thoughts influence your emotions and behaviors. For example, they can fuel a sense of insecurity or confidence, or influence whether or not you seek support from others. Given this, it is helpful to consider how you think about yourself, your body, and how others perceive you.

Self-Reflection Exercise: Self-Consciousness and Your Body

I encourage you to take some time to think about these questions about self-consciousness and your body and write out your responses in your journal.

- What types of situations trigger you to feel self-conscious, anxious, embarrassed, or down?
- What specific thoughts do you have in these situations?
- What emotions are associated with these thoughts?
- What thoughts do you have about your body or physical appearance?
- What emotions come up when thinking about your body or physical appearance?
- Do you wish you could change your body or physical appearance in some way? If so, how?
- Do you wish you could hide your body, or do you try to hide your body? If so, how?
- What thoughts do you have about how others see you, including how they view your body or physical appearance?
- On a scale of 0 to 10, with 0 being not at all and 10 being extremely, how concerned are you about what others think about you?
- How often do you think about how others see you?
- Do you worry that others will negatively judge you? If so, what specific worries do you have?

Changing How You Relate to Your Thoughts

All day, every day, we have thoughts running through our minds. Some of these thoughts are important, meaningful, accurate, or help-ful; some are nonsense; and some are somewhere in between. Many of our thoughts are ingrained, automatic, and frequent. They play in our minds like nonstop chatter that we may or may not notice, and they can have a lot of power over our emotions and behaviors.[5] We tend to automatically believe whatever we are thinking. Our default belief is, *I'm thinking it, so it must be true.* Cognitive fusion is the tendency to believe the literal meaning of thoughts, feelings, and body sensations.[6] We don't see our thoughts as thoughts but as truth. For example, if you think, *I am worthless,* your automatic instinct is to take this thought as a fact rather than simply words that are in your mind. And thinking your worthlessness is a fact will influence how you feel and how you act.

While your thoughts can be accurate at times, thoughts by nature tend to be at least partially skewed, imbalanced, and inaccurate because they are based on your own experiences and worldview. We all have different lenses through which we see the world, and our unique lens impacts what we think and pay attention to. How you interpret and understand yourself, others, and the broader world around you depends on your unique lens or core beliefs. For example, suppose two people see an acquaintance at a coffee shop, and the acquaintance does not say hello or acknowledge them. One person may think, *They don't like me,* based on the belief that they are unlikeable or not good enough, and the other person may think, *They must be really busy today.* All of us are prone to making thinking errors, such as thinking in an extreme, absolute, or categorical manner, which maintain negative beliefs about ourselves, our experiences, and the future.[7]

It is difficult to view situations broadly and objectively. We tend to zoom in on certain aspects of a situation and filter out other aspects, based on our lens and our mood. For example, feeling anxious or depressed distorts thinking and can lead to certain types of thoughts, such as thinking a situation is more dangerous than it is, or thinking you are incompetent.[8] Further, we all have automatic and common thinking habits, and we will think the same type of thought repeatedly based on habit. Yet just because a thought is habitual does not mean it is accurate or helpful. For example, automatic negative thoughts play a role in the emergence of anxiety and depression.[9] And negative self-thinking has been found to occur automatically and frequently and is related to self-esteem. Research suggests that more frequent and habitual negative thinking contributes to lower self-esteem and may hinder positive emotion.[10]

This leads me to one of my favorite phrases in therapy: "Just because you think it doesn't mean it's true." This is a helpful phrase because it is a reminder that you have all sorts of thoughts, and many, if not most, of them are inaccurate, at least partially. Yes, your thoughts can feel true, particularly when they are attached to strong emotions such as anxiety, and that does not mean they are true. Also, it is important to keep in mind that emotions may increase the intensity of and belief in your thoughts, which in turn can fuel the intensity of emotions leading you to get caught in a vicious cycle. By practicing pausing and reminding yourself "Just because I think it doesn't mean it's true," you can stop this cycle from amplifying and continuing.

Inaccurate thoughts are not problematic by themselves. It is when you allow your thoughts to dictate your behavior in problematic ways that you run into difficulty. Let's say I am focused on the thought, *This pain is awful! It is never going to get better,* which leads me to feel sad and irritated, which, in turn, leads me to verbally snap at my partner or a friend. The thought by itself is not problematic. It is natural to have such a thought. It is the focus on the thought and allowing it to influence my behavior in an unhelpful way, snapping at my partner, that is unhelpful.

Many of my clients tell me they want to get rid of their automatic unhelpful thoughts. I appreciate this notion. These thoughts can be troublemakers. The truth is, you have little control over the automatic thoughts that pop into your mind.[11] Thoughts just pop up whether you want them to or not. What you have control over is how you relate and respond to your thoughts once you notice them. In the example above, if I thought, *This pain is awful! It is never going to get better,* and then I paused, noticed and named the thought and my emotions, took a few slow breaths, and practiced being compassionate with myself or connecting with others—placing a hand on my chest and telling myself this is a moment of difficulty, or speaking to my partner in a calm tone of voice—I am helpfully relating to the thought, and it is not problematic. I talk more about how to cope with thoughts or behaviors that feel stuck in chapter 5.

Changing how you relate to your thoughts takes practice. We tend to automatically react to our thoughts in several common and unhelpful ways, including overly focusing on them, which can lead to getting caught in a mental spiral, spinning over and over again on our unhelpful thoughts and fueling the intensity of emotions such as sadness and anxiety, and, again, impulsively allowing our thoughts to impact our behavior in unhelpful ways, including ways that go against our goals and values.

Here's another example: Let's say I value relationships and nature, and based on these values, I set the goal of walking with a friend outside once a week. Before I leave to go on the walk I think, *This pain is so horrible! Why won't it go away?* which leads me to text my friend to cancel the walk and spend the rest of the day on my couch. The behaviors of canceling the walk and spending the rest of the day on the couch are misaligned with my values of relationships and nature, which is ultimately going to decrease my sense of contentment and quality of life. So, it would have been more helpful to acknowledge my thoughts and assess my pain level, and if the pain feels unpleasant yet is not at a high level, go on the walk anyway. In other words, not allow my thoughts to dictate my behavior. You can have whatever thoughts you have and engage in helpful and values-based behaviors.

Of course, keep in mind that it is important to pay attention to your body's needs and listen to your body. In the above example, if my pain was elevated, and resting is the most helpful thing to do, perhaps I could connect with my friend over the phone instead of walking, or reschedule the walk knowing that I am still living my values overall, even if I can't take a walk right now. The aim is to engage in helpful behaviors flexibly, not to ignore your body or rigidly push yourself.

To relate to your thoughts differently, you must first notice and name the thoughts deliberately. Remember, your thoughts can play in your mind like background music that you don't really pay attention to.

Step 1: Notice and name your thought as a thought in a curious, nonjudgmental, and matter-of-fact manner. Pause and complete the following sentence, saying the specific words you are thinking to yourself: "I'm having the thought that . . ." For example, you may say to yourself, "I am having the thought that no one at this party will like me." Or, "I am having the thought that I am incompetent." Or, "I am having the thought that my pain is ruining my life." The aim is to talk to yourself in a kind and curious tone of voice. This is not meant to be an opportunity to be self-critical or speak to yourself in a harsh tone.

Step 2: Name the unhelpful thought habit you may be engaging in. There are several common unhelpful thinking habits that people engage in. These are common ways of thinking that are often default modes of the mind. For example, engaging in all-or-nothing thinking where you think in extreme terms of believing something or someone can be only good or bad, right or wrong, rather than anything in between. Or, thinking in terms of shoulds and musts, thinking or saying, "I should" (or shouldn't), and "I must" puts pressure on yourself and may create unrealistic expectations.

One of my other favorite phrases in therapy is "Stop shoulding on yourself," which speaks to the unhelpfulness of thinking in terms of should. By specifically naming the type of unhelpful thought you are having, you build awareness of your frequent thoughts, which provides more opportunity to relate to your thoughts differently. See the section "Common Unhelpful Thinking Habits" at the end of this chapter. It's a helpful reference sheet to use when you are starting to practice noticing and naming your unhelpful thinking habits. For example, you may say to yourself, "I am having the thought that I am incompetent, and that is a judgment." I would encourage you to take a photograph of "Common Unhelpful Thinking Habits" on your phone so you can easily, and frequently, pull it out and use it.

Step 3: Create mental space from your thoughts. Once you have noticed and named your thoughts, one technique you can practice is creating mental space from your thoughts by practicing letting them come and go. For example, you can practice imagining your mind as the sky and your thoughts as clouds, and let your thought clouds drift by in the sky at their own pace. Below are more examples of how you can practice letting your thoughts come and go. This is a helpful step because it is natural for our thoughts to be sticky. They stick in our minds like a piece of Velcro, and we tend to think about them over and over again, which increases our distress. Another way you can create mental space from your thoughts is to name the thought as a thought, as described above. You can practice this by using the phrase "I'm having the thought that . . ." before stating your thought. This helps you acknowledge the thought as a thought and not a statement of absolute truth that you need to pay attention to, listen to, or act according to.

Using imagery, like imagining your thoughts as clouds in the sky, is a helpful way to practice creating mental space from your thoughts. In addition to thinking of your thoughts as clouds that drift by in the sky, you can imagine sitting in front of a TV or the large screen in a movie theater and imagine that your thoughts are like the credits at the end of a movie. See them on the screen and then just let them scroll up the screen. Or you can imagine standing at a luggage carousel at an airport and imagine you can take your thoughts and place them on the carousel like a suitcase and just let them move down the carousel. Or you can imagine yourself sitting by a stream and placing each thought you have on a leaf and letting it float down the stream. Or imagine you are sitting in a house with both a front and back door, and both doors are open. Your thoughts are like guests that come in the front door and then eventually go out the back door.

The idea is to use any image that is helpful to you and allows you to practice letting your thoughts come and go. Note that you are not using the image as a way to push your thoughts away. Rather, you are simply letting them pass by at whatever pace they want to move at, and they will likely pop up again. That is okay. Just keep letting them come and go.

Step 4: Challenge your thoughts. Once you have noticed and named your thoughts, another helpful technique is to directly challenge your thoughts by asking yourself questions that examine the accuracy or helpfulness of the thoughts. Remember, automatic thoughts tend to be unbalanced and inaccurate, and we often don't realize that. We take them at face value and think, *This must be true.* So, it can be helpful to slow down and practice directly examining and challenging your thoughts, which creates more objectivity. See the section "Challenging Unhelpful Automatic Thoughts" at the end of this chapter. It lists questions you can use to challenge your thoughts. Feel free to test out several of these questions on your thoughts and see which ones are most helpful to you.

Step 5: Create more balanced and helpful alternative thoughts. Challenging your thoughts may help you realize that your thoughts tend to be inaccurate, unbalanced, and unhelpful. Once you have this awareness, you can create more balanced and helpful thoughts that you can repeat to yourself each time your unhelpful automatic thoughts pop up. For example, if I fall, my automatic thought might be, *This is so embarrassing! Everyone around me is going to think I am awkward and clumsy.* By practicing the steps above, I can mentally take a step back and notice that this thought is an emotional reasoning and mind-reading type of thought that is unbalanced and unhelpful, and it leads me to feel increased embarrassment and insecurity. I can challenge it by listing things that my body is capable of, or listing things about myself that I am proud of. Then I may create the alternative thought of, *My body doesn't move like most bodies. That is okay. Falling does not make me awkward.* The aim is to create a balanced thought that feels authentic to you, not necessarily a positive thought. For some people, it feels more helpful and authentic to focus on creating neutral thoughts versus positive ones, especially if they are not feeling positive about a situation. Once you have created a more balanced and helpful alternative thought, it is important to repeat, repeat, repeat it each time an unhelpful automatic thought arises. Automatic thoughts tend to be ingrained, and repetition helps strengthen more helpful thoughts.

I have included a "Thought Record" tool at the end of this chapter that you can use to write down your automatic thoughts along with more helpful alternative thoughts. It is useful to write down automatic thoughts as doing so allows you to see your thoughts more objectively and to more fully process and practice the skills of noticing, naming, and challenging your thoughts.

Writing down thoughts can also help you manage worry. Worry is a natural response to uncertainty, yet excessive worry can intensify anxiety and distress. **Scheduled worry time** is a skill used to manage consistent and intrusive worry and teaches you that worry does not require your immediate attention whenever it pops up.[12] To practice scheduled worry time, schedule a daily time of between five and thirty minutes to worry. Do not practice for longer than thirty minutes as doing so can encourage excessive worry. For example, your worry time might be daily from 6 to 6:15 p.m. Set a timer, and during that time, briefly write down all of your concerns, worries, and problems. You can do this by taking out a piece of paper and drawing a vertical line down the middle of the page. On the left side of the line, briefly list out all of your concerns, and on the right side of the line next to each concern, list one small step you can take to work toward problem-solving the concern. For example, maybe it would be helpful to email a colleague about a work concern you have. You don't need to resolve your entire concern, just write down one small step you can take to work on it.

If you are worried about something you cannot control, or there is no concrete step to take, write down a coping skill that would help you manage stress or anxiety, such as deep breathing, taking a short walk, or calling a friend. When the timer goes off, deliberately remind yourself that your concerns are on the page and you do not need to hold them in your mind. When you start worrying at times outside your scheduled worry time, tell yourself you can come back to your concerns during the next scheduled worry time and practice moving forward with your day.

Cognitive Defusion

Creating mental space from your thoughts, which is described in step 3 above, is beneficial. The technical term for this skill is cognitive defusion, which is a core clinical process in acceptance and commitment therapy (ACT).[13] Cognitive defusion means "de-fusing" or distancing from unhelpful patterns of thinking. The idea is that we all tend to overidentify with our thoughts, amplifying them in our minds to become "the truth." When we become attached or fused to thoughts in this way, they become powerful and can lead us to act in unhelpful ways. Cognitive defusion techniques involve recognizing the process of thinking, that thoughts are transient, and that thoughts are not necessarily true.[14] These techniques create separation between your thoughts and your behaviors, and allow unhelpful thoughts to arise without behaving in unhelpful ways.

Thoughts are just thoughts. This statement is not meant to minimize the emotional impact that thoughts can have or to negate the information associated with thoughts. These are both valid. The point is that language and words often fall short of accurately representing reality, and thoughts are no more powerful than we allow them to be. They are words and pictures that float through our minds. We are the ones who give them meaning.

The skill of cognitive defusion helps you to relate differently to bothersome thoughts. Just because you "have a thought" does not mean that an action must be taken. When thoughts seem frightening or powerful, there is a sense of urgency associated with them that may prompt you to jump into action. When thoughts pop into your mind or when you have thoughts that you cannot get out of your mind, it is helpful to practice taking a mental step back by noticing and observing thoughts before taking any action. The general aim of cognitive defusion is to reduce the influence of unhelpful thoughts on behavior and to practice being mindful of the present moment and aware of your experience.

Practicing creating mental space from your thoughts enables you to respond to your thoughts in a manner that facilitates helpful behavior versus automatically allowing the thought to dictate your behavior. A helpful behavior may be the opposite of what your automatic thought is telling you to do. For example, if you have a goal of spending time with friends and tell yourself, *I feel too tired to be around other people,* whenever you think about scheduling time with friends, this thought will lead you to not reach out to friends. Practicing cognitive defusion allows you to see this thought as a thought and realize that it may not be true, or not completely true, and also not helpful, and if spending time with friends is important to you, it is beneficial to find realistic and doable ways of doing so.

When practicing cognitive defusion, you understand that

- Thoughts are merely sounds, words, stories, and bits of language passing through your mind.

- Thoughts may or may not be true. You don't automatically believe them.

- Thoughts may or may not be important or helpful. You pay attention only if they're helpful.

- Thoughts are not orders. You don't have to obey them.

- Thoughts may or may not be wise. You don't automatically follow their advice.[15]

In addition to what is noted above in step 3, here are some additional ways you can practice cognitive defusion:

- Give your mind a name. For example, "There goes Bob the Bully talking nonstop again."

- Say thoughts in a silly voice, or sing them aloud.

- Imagine thoughts as junk email—you may get the email, but you don't have to read it.

- Imagine thoughts as pop-up ads on the internet that you can close.

- Picture a sandy shoreline, and visualize your thoughts written in the sand, then watch the waves gently wash them away.

- Imagine yourself sitting in the passenger side of a car that is driving down a highway and watch your thoughts pass by on billboards.

Common Unhelpful Thinking Habits

- **Mental Filter:** Noticing or focusing on whatever your filter wants you to and dismissing anything that doesn't fit. Usually, the filter is negative. For example, focusing on the one perceived negative thing that happened that day instead of the five things that went well.

- **Judgments:** Making judgments or evaluations about yourself, others, events, or the world rather than describing what you see and have evidence for.

- **Mind-Reading:** Assuming you know what other people are thinking, particularly as it relates to you. For example, *They think I am incompetent.*

- **Emotional Reasoning:** Thinking how you feel matches the reality of a situation. For example, *I feel anxious, so I must be in danger.*

- **Prediction:** Believing you know what is going to happen in the future. For example, *I won't be able to go to the event next week because my pain will be too bad.*

- **Mountains and Molehills:** Exaggerating the good and positive aspects of others or a situation and minimizing your own positive attributes. Or exaggerating an objectively minor problem or challenge. For example, a friend is fifteen minutes late meeting you and you think, *They must not care about me. I guess we won't be friends anymore.*

- **Compare and Despair:** Seeing only the good and positive aspects of others and comparing yourself negatively against them. For example, *That person is so capable and skilled. I have no skills or talents and don't measure up.*

- **Catastrophizing:** Imagining and believing the worst possible thing will happen. For example, *My fatigue is so bad that I will never be able to go out with friends again!*

- **Critical Self:** Self-criticism, putting yourself down, or blaming yourself for events and situations that are not your responsibility (or not your total responsibility).

- **All-or-Nothing Thinking:** Thinking that something or someone can only be good or bad, right or wrong, rather than anything in between. For example, *Any day that I have pain is a bad day.*

- **Shoulds and Musts:** Thinking or saying, "I should" (or shouldn't) and "I must" puts pressure on yourself and may create unrealistic expectations. For example, *I should move my body every day.*

- **Memories:** Current situations and events can trigger upsetting memories, leading you to think that the danger is here and now rather than in the past, which can cause distress in the present moment.

Challenging Unhelpful Automatic Thoughts

- What evidence supports this thought? What evidence does not support this thought?

- Could there be any other explanations?

- Is this thought accurate? Is it 100 percent accurate?

- Is this thought accurate or helpful, or am I thinking it based on habit?

- What is the worst that could happen? The best? The most realistic?

- If the worst thing were to happen, how bad would that be? How would I cope with it?

- Do I know for certain that _____ will happen?

- Am I 100 percent sure about this?

- Does _____ have to lead to or equal _____?

- Is _____ really so important or consequential?

- Does _____'s opinion really reflect that of everyone else?

- What is the effect of believing my automatic thought? What is the effect of taking a different perspective on this situation?

- How useful is it for me to be focusing on this thought?

- Is there a helpful action I can take to help me problem-solve or cope with this situation?

- What would I tell a friend if they were in the same situation?

- If I must be in this situation, how can I cope with it?

- What wisdom can I gain from this situation to deal with similar circumstances in the future?

Thought Record

Situation	Mood/ emotions Rate intensity 0–10	Physical sensations	Automatic unhelpful thought	Alternate more balanced and helpful thought	Helpful behavior or coping skill Rerate intensity 0–10
What happened?	What emotions did I feel? How intense were they?	What did I notice in my body?	What went through my mind? What specific thoughts did I have?	What's another way to think about this? Use "Challenging Unhelpful Automatic Thoughts" above.	What is a helpful action for me to take? After taking that action, what is the intensity level of my emotions?

CHAPTER FIVE

Engage the Power of the Present to Get Unstuck

THERE ARE MANY THINGS in life that I do not have control over. I have no control over, and can't change, that I have cerebral palsy. It just is. It creates certain challenges in my daily life, such as chronic pain and fatigue, and while I can practice helpful coping skills and feel less held back by these challenges, I can't fully get rid of them. Numerous factors are often out of our control or related to larger societal issues that can create major problems for people, such as injustice, discrimination, prejudice, and a variety of additional societal and environmental issues. For example, disabled people are unemployed or underemployed at higher rates than nondisabled people,[1] and research with African American women has shown that persistent racial discrimination predicts inflammation, which in turn predicts the number of chronic diseases a person has.[2] Similarly, research with Asian Americans has shown that reports of discrimination were associated with an increased number of chronic health conditions after controlling for variables such as age, education, employment, income, and relationship status.[3]

Further, research demonstrates that discrimination in the health care system has been associated with negative mental and physical health outcomes for patients. People with chronic health conditions, such as heart disease and diabetes, who have been discriminated against are often less engaged in health care. Patient reports of discrimination are common among racial and ethnic minority groups and are associated with reports of worse health, lower satisfaction with health care, and lower utilization of health services.[4]

With certain concerns, such as stress, anxiety, depression, or chronic pain, it is not necessarily the concern itself, or the concern in isolation, that is problematic, though it may be unpleasant and challenging to experience, but how we choose to relate to the concern that is unhelpful. We can add fuel to the fire, increase our distress, and potentially create suffering based on how we relate to our thoughts and feelings and the behaviors we choose to engage in.

I have had to learn, often through increased distress, to recognize when I am cognitively and behaviorally stuck, repeating the same unhelpful thoughts or behaviors, and to get out of my own way by changing my behavior and doing something differently. In psychology, being stuck refers to a state of arrest or being thwarted that creates emotional and psychological distress, or the experience that your current skills are inadequate to meet the demands of your current circumstances.[5] In practice, I help myself get unstuck by accepting the present moment reality, even if I don't like it, and challenging myself to implement helpful coping skills and change unhelpful behaviors, even if I don't feel like it and even if it is difficult. This is way easier said than done. And I am often in my own way by stewing in my stuckness. For example, I can easily become mentally stuck on how much I don't like a certain physical sensation, or think the same unhelpful thought over and over, such as *This is so frustrating. Why do I have to be in pain all the time? Why is my back (or legs, or shoulders) constantly hurting?* This leads to increased distress and an ongoing sense of stuckness. Stuckness is demoralizing. It sucks the sense of capability, confidence, and hope out of us. It makes us want to stay in bed with a blanket over our heads, literally or figuratively.

We all get cognitively, emotionally, or behaviorally stuck. We fixate on the same thoughts repeatedly, feel trapped and overwhelmed by certain emotions, or repeat the same behaviors even when we know they are detrimental. Why does this happen? Why do we continue thinking or doing things that we know are unhelpful? There are many reasons you can get, and stay, stuck. Barriers to behavior change include lack of knowledge, not knowing how to effectively change behavior, low self-efficacy or feeling incapable of making a helpful change, and valuing the current unhelpful behavior over a potentially more helpful one.[6]

Change is challenging and often scary. It takes energy and effort, and perhaps you don't know where to start, don't want to put forth the effort, are doubtful of your ability to make a change, are unsure of the meaning and purpose behind a change, or feel scared about not knowing where change will lead. Also, there is a strong sense of familiarity that can come from repeated patterns, of doing things the same way, even if it's unhelpful. Research suggests that people seek out the familiar because familiarity is comforting and therefore can be enjoyable.[7] Yet it is possible to get unstuck, to create options and a greater sense of psychological flexibility.

Acceptance and commitment therapy (ACT) defines *psychological flexibility* as the ability to connect with the present moment, being aware of thoughts and emotions without trying to change them, be controlled by them, or allow them to dictate behavior, and depending on the situation, sticking with or changing behavior for it to align with personal values.[8]

Self-Reflection Exercise: Psychological Flexibility

I encourage you to take some time to think about these questions about psychological flexibility and write out your responses in your journal.

+ In a given day, how much time do you spend thinking about the past or the future?

+ Do you notice yourself dwelling on the past or future? If so, are there certain thoughts, images, or ideas that feel difficult to mentally move on from?

+ Do you feel disconnected from, or unsure of, your thoughts, feelings, or behaviors? Does it feel like you are going through the motions of the day yet don't really know what you are thinking, feeling, or doing?

- Do you have "sticky thoughts" that you tend to overly focus on? For example, rigid rules or expectations of yourself or others, including how you or others should act or feel, criticisms or judgments, set reasons why you can or cannot do certain things, and so on. If so, write out examples of these thoughts.

- Do you try to avoid certain thoughts, feelings, or physical sensations? If so, what specifically do you avoid and how do you try to avoid it? For example, do you try not to feel your physical pain by spending a lot of time on your phone?

- How do you see yourself as a person? In other words, how do you define yourself, and how would you talk about yourself to others? For example, do you see yourself as broken or damaged or strong and capable? Are you defining yourself rigidly, and is your sense of self fluid and changeable, or does it seem fixed?

- What are your core values? See "Values" in chapter 6 for guidance. Do you feel clear and certain about your values, or do you feel unclear about them? Are you acting consistently or inconsistently with your values? In other words, do your daily behaviors align with your larger values?

- In general, are you currently engaging in unhelpful behaviors that are impulsive, avoidant, or self-defeating? If so, what are the specific behaviors you are engaging in?

Your responses to these questions will provide insight into your current degree of psychological flexibility. If you are generally connected to the present moment, aware of your thoughts, feelings, and behaviors without feeling consumed by them, and engaging in behaviors that are helpful and meaningful, you are likely psychologically flexible. If you suspect that you are psychologically inflexible, the skills below will support increasing your flexibility.

Being caught in your thoughts, like an insect trapped in a spider's web, is one way you can become stuck and psychologically inflexible. When you are caught in your thoughts, you are disconnected from the present moment and miss out on opportunities to do things you find meaningful and important. One way you can connect with the present moment is by practicing mindfulness. Mindfulness skills help you to notice and observe your thoughts, feelings, and physical sensations nonjudgmentally without getting overly focused or fixated on them. For example, if I am feeling anxious, I may practice saying to myself, "I am experiencing anxiety right now," or "I am having the thought that others will think I am incapable," without adding judgments to my experience—"This is so horrible! I can't feel this way!"— and then deliberately shift my attention to the present moment instead of getting caught in my thoughts or feelings. For example, I practice focusing on the sensation of my breath moving in and out of my body and using the breath to anchor my attention to the present moment. I'll share some additional mindfulness practices later in this chapter.

A flexible material can bend, move, or flex without being damaged or breaking. Similarly, a component of psychological flexibility is being adaptable with your behavior, and being able to change behavior (in other words, do something differently) when doing so is helpful. At the same time, flexibility can also mean sticking with a personally meaningful and important behavior even when doing so is difficult. Being aware of your values (see "Values" in chapter 6) helps support flexible and helpful behavior by making change more worthwhile because it is based on what you find valuable. Changing behavior is challenging, and it is easier to change behavior or persist in making a helpful change when doing so matches your values. We feel more motivated when behavior is personally meaningful and not based on a "should" thought or what someone else wants us to do.

Getting Unstuck

When we feel stuck, we feel incapable of making a change and are often waiting for an external event to happen that will improve or resolve our problems. This mentality is summed up by when-then or if-then thinking. When-then thinking is a thought pattern of putting off doing, being, or possibly feeling a certain way until a particular set of circumstances happens. "When I have more time, then I will start the hobby I have been thinking about." "When I am less anxious, then I will take a trip." "When my pain is better, then I will go for a walk." "When I am not depressed, then I will see my friend." "When I feel better about my appearance, then I will go to the party." Being in a state of waiting, particularly waiting for something that is out of your control, at least to some degree, and that is not going to magically happen, is often the same as being stuck.

This is not to deny the existence of legitimate barriers to taking action. Real barriers do exist, and it is important to acknowledge these barriers and what you can control, and be realistic about what type of action is most feasible. For example, perhaps you lack information about what a helpful change may look like or how to modify an activity so that it fits your physical abilities and needs, and you lack confidence in your ability to change. Perhaps you lack time, money, social support, child care, or other resources that would support a change, or you experience discrimination that impedes taking action.[9] And waiting to act often means not living the life you want to live, now, in the present moment. Ideal circumstances do not exist. External circumstances may not change, and even if they do, that does not necessarily mean you will feel differently or other barriers will not arise.

So it's usually not easy, and one way you can get unstuck is to start small and start now. What is one small step you can take now to shift your behavior and possibly feel less stuck? Again, small changes are helpful. You do not need to make a large change to experience a beneficial impact. For example, maybe you could call a friend, schedule a meal out with a loved one, go for a walk, listen to a meditation exercise, practice slow, deep breathing, set a timer for fifteen minutes and start a task you have been putting off, and so on. If pain, fatigue, or other factors are limiting your ability to engage in an activity, you may be able to modify it to better fit your needs in the moment. For example, if you like to paint yet are feeling too fatigued to get out your painting materials, perhaps you could color in a coloring book or simply doodle with paper and pen. If you have the desire to move your body and are unable to walk, perhaps you could do some seated shoulder rolls or gently lift your arms up and down.

Some additional ways you can get unstuck:

- Nonjudgmentally notice and name thoughts you are having, which may include when-then or if-then thinking.

- Revisit the "Changing How You Relate to Your Thoughts" skills in chapter 4 to help determine whether your thoughts are helpful in the moment. For example, are you engaging in a common unhelpful thinking habit? If so, practice naming the habit and using the "Challenging Unhelpful Automatic Thoughts" questions in chapter 4 to examine your thoughts and reframe them to be more balanced.

- Use the cognitive defusion skills in chapter 4 to create mental distance from your thoughts so they have less influence on your behaviors.

- Practice the radical acceptance skills in chapter 3 to help you come to terms with circumstances as they are in the moment so you are not using energy resisting what already is or what you cannot change. Then, you can put your energy toward controllable and values-based action.

- Ask yourself, and write down, how your current behavior does or does not align with your values and what you are hoping to achieve moving forward.

- Set a small, realistic, and values-based goal. Small actions accumulate, help you build a sense of momentum, and allow you to start feeling unstuck. See "Helpful Goals Are SMART" on the next page.

Setting goals helps increase motivation and facilitates behavior change. Research has suggested that for goals to be motivating, they must be specific or have a focused target, be challenging yet attainable, and be created and accepted by you rather than someone else telling you what to do.[10] It is also helpful to set specific intentions about where, when, and how you will achieve a goal as research shows that considering when a behavior will occur sets the stage for implementing the behavior.[11] SMART goals are goals that are specific, measurable, achievable, relevant, and time-bound. Using a SMART framework helps to create specific and realistic goals, and in therapy, it is a respectful and collaborative way for a therapist to offer guidance and aid a client in setting and meeting personally relevant goals.[12]

Helpful Goals Are SMART

S—specific: The most helpful goals are clear and specific. People often create goals that are too general, which can lead to difficulty getting started, as it may be unclear where to start. So get specific! What exactly will you do?

M—measurable: How will you measure or track your goal? How will you know if you are making progress or have completed your goal?

A—achievable: Is your goal achievable, attainable, and realistic given your current resources, circumstances, and abilities? If your goal seems too big or unrealistic, how can you break it into smaller, more doable pieces?

R—relevant: Why is this goal important or meaningful to you? Why do you want to do it? Does it align with your larger values? The more relevant and meaningful the goal, often the more motivated you will be to do it and the more possibility there is that acting on the goal will enhance your quality of life.

T—time-bound: How long will you work on this goal—one week, one month? Is it short-term or ongoing? When do you want to check in on your progress and make changes to your goal as needed? Even if your goal is long-term, it is helpful to check in and ask yourself how you are doing along the way so you can pivot as needed.

My Goal Is

Take some time to think about your current goals. Are there specific behaviors you want to change or engage in? For example, are there activities you have been wanting to do or certain behaviors that may enhance your sense of well-being or quality of life? The below questions will help you create a SMART goal. Feel free to create as many SMART goals as you want, and keep in mind it may be helpful to focus on one goal at a time.

S: What do I want to do or achieve? Be specific.

M: How will I know I reached my goal? How will I track it?

A: Is this goal realistic for me? What resources do I need to achieve it?

R: Why is this goal meaningful to me? Does it support my larger values?

T: How long do I plan to implement this goal? When will I check my progress?

Here is an example of a SMART goal for practicing mindful breathing.

S: I will practice mindful breathing for five minutes, at around 1 p.m., on Mondays and Wednesdays (twice a week).

M: I will make a note on my phone each time I practice mindful breathing and will set a reminder on my phone to check my progress each Sunday to see if I practiced twice that week.

A: This goal seems realistic, and the main resource I need is time. I can cut down my goal to once a week on Mondays as needed.

R: This goal is meaningful to me as it will help me slow down and be present. It is related to my larger values of presence and connection.

T: I will initially practice for two weeks and check in on my progress each Sunday to see how it is going. If I am not hitting my goal, I will plan to change my goal to practicing for five minutes, once a week on Mondays, and then check in again after another two weeks.

Being Mindful

Mindfulness is the practice of bringing direct, intentional, and non-judgmental awareness to the present moment and what you are doing while you are doing it. It is the practice of tuning in to what's going on in your mind and body, and the outside world, moment to moment.[13] Mindfulness can allow you to notice more objectively and nonjudgmentally what is happening in the moment versus what your automatic thoughts or emotions may be telling you is happening. The aim of practicing mindfulness exercises is not to change how you feel or to lessen stress, anxiety, or depression. The aim is to practice tuning in to the present moment and your direct experience rather than solely thinking about your experience.

At the same time, it can be the case that you can change your experience by changing how you pay attention to and relate to it. Practicing mindfulness creates options for how you relate to your experience, particularly to unpleasant emotions and experiences, as mindfulness cultivates curiosity and acceptance of uncomfortable experiences.[14] For example, if I am feeling physical pain or feeling anxious, I can practice nonjudgmentally noticing and observing this experience rather than automatically trying to avoid or decrease it. This may look like naming my experience in the moment without judging it as bad or negative, noticing my physical sensations, and making room for them by breathing into the sensations and imagining creating space for them as I breathe. For example, if my back is hurting, I may say to myself, "My lower back is hurting." I then nonjudgmentally observe and describe the pain sensations: "I'm noticing a throbbing ache that has a pulsing quality to it," and intentionally breathe, not to try to get rid of the pain, but to make room for the pain. I do this by imagining that I am sending my breath directly to my lower back (the part of my body that hurts) and that as I breathe my body is gently expanding and making room for the pain to be there, as if I have a big balloon in my torso that is slowly inflating.

It is easy to become caught up in unhelpful thoughts and mentally spin repeatedly as if you are in a mental washing machine. Mindfulness allows you to practice deliberately directing your attention to your experience in the present moment versus being stuck in your head. Our minds are really good at thinking about the past or the future. You can think of this as mental time travel. Mental time travel is the ability to think about situations that have already happened or imagine fictitious events that may take place in the future. When you are engaged in mental time travel, you are disconnected from your external environment and the present moment.[15]

It can be helpful to deliberately and purposely think about the past or future so that you can learn from your behavior and plan for future events. Yet, it is problematic when your mind is thinking about the past or future in a nondeliberate and spinning manner, thinking about the same thing over and over without a helpful outcome. This type of mental spinning, or rumination (repeated, prolonged, and recurrent negative thinking) can lead to increased stress, exhaustion, irritability, anxiety, and depression.[16] For example, if you are living with chronic pain and have an upcoming social event that requires you to be more physically active than is typical, you may feel anticipatory anxiety about experiencing increased pain, which leads you to excessively worry about the event and imagine worst-case scenarios.

Mindfulness helps you to settle your mind. The aim is not to stop your mind from wandering or engaging in mental time travel. Rather, the aim is to recognize when this is happening and gently bring your attention back to the present moment. Ultimately, mindfulness can help create a greater sense of ease in your daily life because it helps you learn to slow down, tune in to your direct experience, and deliberately choose how you want to respond in any given moment, which can save you energy in the long run and increase your quality of life, versus automatically defaulting to your habitual reactions, which may be unhelpful.

Further, practicing mindfulness allows you to shift from doing mode to being mode.[17] Most of us are in doing mode as we go about our lives. We jump from task to task trying to get things done, often not fully paying attention to what is in front of us. Doing mode is about thinking, problem-solving, and meeting goals. This approach is helpful when there is a specific external task that you need to complete, and it can be problematic and create distress when you use doing mode with your internal experience. This relates to acceptance and how, if you are stuck in doing mode and focused on fixing, resisting, or struggling with your internal experience, you can create a sense of suffering and block helpful behaviors.[18] When you are in being mode, you are aware, tuned in to the moment, and make intentional choices (versus default to habits). You connect with life directly with your senses (versus thinking about life), you are focused on the here and now, you practice being interested in and curious about your full experience, not just the pleasant parts, and you allow yourself and your experience to be as it is in the moment (versus demanding it be different). You see thoughts as thoughts—as mental events that enter and leave your mind, and you value what is happening now (versus solely focusing on a future goal).

Mindfulness is centered in being mode, and one of the intentions of mindfulness is to notice when you are in doing mode or being mode and to switch as useful. Keep in mind that mindfulness takes practice, and it is worth repeating that the aim of mindfulness is not to keep your mind from wandering. It is to recognize when you are on a mental train that is unintentionally and unhelpfully taking you to the past or the future and coming back to the present. You will likely have to practice this repeatedly, perhaps as frequently as every few minutes. That is okay. You are not aiming to achieve a set outcome such as feeling calm or having a clear and focused mind. The process of practice itself is helpful, and over time, with consistent practice, you may find it is a bit easier to more fully attend to the present moment. In the following sections, you'll find a few of my favorite brief mindfulness exercises.

Notice and Name

Throughout this book, I have talked about the helpfulness of noticing and naming your internal experience. This skill is fundamental to many other skills because it enables you to pause, slow down, and tune in to your experience and what is happening inside your mind and body at any moment, including when you are having distressing thoughts, emotions, or physical sensations. By pausing and tuning in to what you are thinking and feeling, you create the option of using other useful coping skills and engaging in purposeful and helpful behaviors.

To practice this important skill, a few times per day, perhaps around mealtimes, or once every hour or two, pause and nonjudgmentally notice your thoughts, feelings, and physical sensations, whether they are pleasant, unpleasant, or neutral. Remember, nonjudgmental observation involves not judging your experience, for example, not judging it as bad or negative. Then, practice naming your experience. You can do this by completing the following sentences:

+ I am having the thought that _____

+ I am feeling _____

+ My body or specific body part (neck, shoulders, chest, stomach, back) is feeling _____

You may want to review "Tuning In to Internal Experience" in chapter 1 for more tips on noticing and naming your experiences.

STOP Skill

The STOP skill is a brief mindfulness exercise that is helpful to practice when emotional intensity is increasing, when feeling overwhelmed, or when you recognize that it would be helpful to take a moment to ground yourself and be more fully present (versus caught in your head). Research with medical students has suggested that the STOP skill is a simple and flexible way to cultivate mindfulness and enhance a sense of well-being.[19]

Stop and Slow your breathing: Whatever you are doing, simply stop. Take a few slow breaths, and mindfully observe the breath flowing in and flowing out. Notice the physical sensations of your breath as it moves in and out of your body, your chest or belly rising and falling. This will help you to shift out of autopilot mode and connect with the present moment, here and now.

Take note: While staying connected to your breathing, take note of your experience in this moment. Notice what you are thinking, perhaps saying "thinking" to yourself. Notice what you are feeling, and take a moment to name the feelings that are here. Notice any physical sensations in your body. See if you can practice acknowledging and noticing your experience, even if it is unwanted or unpleasant. Practice being curious about your experience rather than judgmental.

Open up: Practice opening to your experience, allowing it to be whatever it is in this moment. See your thoughts, feelings, and physical sensations for what they are—things that come and go—and give them space. Breathe into any sensations of discomfort, tension, or resistance, not to get rid of the sensations, but to practice making room for your experience, holding it in friendly awareness. Try saying to yourself, "It's okay. Whatever it is, it's okay. Let me be open to it."

Proceed mindfully and Pursue your values: Mindfully consider how you would like to move forward in this moment. If it feels helpful, ask yourself, "What is beneficial for me, for others, and for the situation I'm in? How would I like to act, so that I can look back and think my response was helpful?" Going forward, see if you can allow what is most meaningful and important to guide you.

Mindful Breathing

Mindful breathing is the practice of fully tuning in to the sensation of your breath as you breathe, of noticing the air moving in and out of your body. You are observing the feeling of the breath as it first enters your body, noticing the feeling of air entering your nose, observing the feeling of the breath as you continue to inhale and it travels into your lungs, and noticing the feeling of the air leaving your body as you exhale out of your nose or mouth.

Mindful breathing can be related to relaxation breathing exercises, yet is a different practice. With relaxation breathing exercises, you are practicing changing your breathing in some way, by breathing more deeply or slowly, for example, and the aim is to feel more relaxed. With mindful breathing, you are not changing your breathing, you are simply practicing fully observing your breath. Also, the aim is not to relax, which may or may not happen, but to practice paying attention to your breathing and using the sensation of the breath as an anchor to the present moment, something you can use to root yourself in the present moment. With that being said, you may find that as you practice paying attention to your breath, you naturally breathe a bit slower and deeper and feel more relaxed. If you have trouble breathing or use a device to help you breathe, you may still be able to observe the sensation of air coming in and out of your body. I would encourage you to try mindful breathing, and if you find that it does not fit your needs, feel free to leave it.

To practice mindful breathing, settle into a comfortable sitting or lying position, aiming to be engaged in the present moment. You can either close your eyes or pick a spot in front of you to gently look at.

Before focusing on your breath, bring your awareness to the general physical sensations of your body by focusing your attention on the sensations of touch and pressure in your body where it contacts the floor and whatever you are sitting on. Spend a minute or two noticing and observing these sensations.

Now, bring your awareness to the specific physical sensations of your breath as the breath moves in and out of your body. It may be helpful to place one hand on your chest and one hand on your belly to aid in feeling the air moving in and out of your body. Focus your awareness on wherever you notice your breath. It may be in your nose, your chest, your belly, or somewhere else. You may notice the sensations of slight stretching in your chest or belly as it rises with each inhale and then gently collapses with each exhale. As best you can, follow with your awareness the changing physical sensations of your breath as the breath first enters your body on the inhale and all the way through as the breath leaves your body on the exhale, perhaps noticing the slight pauses between one inhale and the following exhale and between one exhale and the following inhale.

There is no need to try to control your breathing in any way—simply let the breath breathe itself. As best you can, also bring this attitude of allowance to the rest of your experience. There is nothing to be fixed, no particular state to be achieved. As best you can, simply allow your experience to be your experience, without needing it to be other than it is.

Sooner or later (usually sooner), your mind will wander away from the focus on the breath to thinking, planning, drifting along—whatever.

This is perfectly okay. It's simply what minds do. It is not a mistake or a failure. When you notice that your awareness is no longer on the breath, briefly acknowledge where your mind has been ("I was thinking"), then gently bring your awareness back to focusing on the physical sensations of the breath moving in and out of the body.

No matter how often you notice your mind has wandered (this will happen over and over again), as best you can, acknowledge your ability to reconnect with your experience in the moment, gently bringing your attention back to the breath, and simply resume awareness of the physical sensations that come with each inhale and exhale.

As best you can, bring a quality of kindness and compassion to your awareness, seeing the repeated wanderings of the mind as opportunities to bring patience and gentle curiosity to your experience.

Continue with the practice for five to ten minutes, or longer if you wish, reminding yourself from time to time that the intention is simply to be aware of your experience in each moment, as best you can. Using the breath as an anchor, gently reconnect with the here and now each time you notice that your mind has wandered and is no longer following the breath.

Welcoming Mindfulness Exercise

Another mindfulness exercise that can help you relate to thoughts, feelings, or physical sensations in a more open, willing, and less resistant manner, which decreases a sense of struggling with your experience, is to practice "welcoming" them and thinking of them as "old friends." Welcoming does not mean you have to like what you are experiencing. It just means you are practicing creating space for your full experience. Thinking of your thoughts, feelings, or sensations as old friends implies that they have likely been around for a while, whether you like it or not, sort of like an annoying family member, and in this way, they are companions. It also implies that your thoughts, feelings, and sensations are usually well-intentioned and trying to be helpful even if they are not.

To engage in the practice of welcoming, get into a comfortable but alert position. If you can, be seated and place both feet on the floor.

Gently close your eyes (you can leave your eyes open if that is more comfortable) and begin by focusing your attention on your breathing.

Notice where your attention goes as you do so. It may go to your nose or to the rise and fall of your chest or belly. Spend these next few moments being aware of your breathing. Follow each breath as you breathe in and out.

Now, as you remain aware of your breathing, following the in-breath and then the out-breath. I would like you to repeat to yourself, silently, on the in-breath, "Welcome pain" (or another thought, emotion, or physical sensation word that seems to fit), and on the out-breath add, "My old friend." Continue to repeat these words as you gently breathe. If you get distracted or caught by a thought, practice bringing your attention back to your breath and the words "Welcome pain, my old friend." Keep practicing for a few minutes, repeating the words "Welcome pain" as you inhale, and "My old friend" as you exhale.

Now gently release your attention from the words and your breath and focus your attention on your body sitting wherever you are. Picture the room in your mind's eye. When you are ready, rejoin the moment by opening your eyes.

CHAPTER SIX

Live Your Values to Enhance Quality of Life

I AM CONSISTENTLY PRACTICING skills to effectively manage my cerebral palsy and enhance my overall well-being physically, mentally, and emotionally. At my core, I consider myself a joyful person. My mom likes to say that I came into the world smiling, and it seems I have been smiling ever since. I think my natural smiley facial expression is related to my internal content nature. I am someone who relishes the seemingly small and simple things in life: the feeling of the sun on my face, my first sip of coffee in the morning, or the pleasure I get from eating a delicious meal. This is not to say that I constantly feel joy and contentment. The fatigue and pain I experience can strip away my joy, at least for a while, which is one of the more emotionally challenging aspects of living with a disability.

As I cope with daily challenges, my goal is to fully acknowledge my lived experience in the moment, including all the difficult pieces, and be joyful. Being joyful is not the same as feeling happy. It means tuning in to the present moment, being grateful for the finite and incredible life I have, being balanced in my thinking and perspective, reminding myself what brings me joy, and spending time cultivating that joy. I do not always do this well. I am regularly focusing on my fatigue and pain, thinking about the aspects of my daily life that feel challenging, difficult, or unfair, or worrying about completing tasks. This is okay to a point. It is important to acknowledge and feel my feelings without pushing them away, and I also do not want to consistently put my fatigue and pain on center stage. Because when I do, I lose my joy. I lose my spark. I lose a key part of my identity and what makes me, me. I am someone who values connection, relationships, and joy. When I am focused on my fatigue and pain, I am less able to connect to myself and others, less invested in nurturing my relation-ships, and less joyful. And ultimately my quality of life is diminished. So, I intentionally shift toward joyfulness, and living my values helps me do that.

Self-Reflection Exercise: Values and Quality of Life

I encourage you to take some time to think about these questions about values and quality of life and write out your responses in your journal.

- ◆ What is important and meaningful to you in life? In other words, what do you value?
- ◆ Do your daily behaviors align with your larger values? If not, where are the gaps?
- ◆ What gets in the way of taking values-based action?
- ◆ When do you feel a sense of vitality or spark?
- ◆ When do you feel most like yourself?
- ◆ On a scale of 0 to 10, with 0 being not at all and 10 being extremely, how satisfied are you with your quality of life overall?
- ◆ If you are not very satisfied, what action could you take to increase your satisfaction? Small, realistic actions are often the most helpful.

Values and Quality of Life

I broadly define quality of life as how satisfied you are with your life overall. There are many components of quality of life, and you may feel high satisfaction in one area of life, for example, relationships, and low satisfaction in another, for example, work. One way to enhance your overall quality of life is to align your daily behaviors with your values—what is meaningful to you; what you care about and consider important. Personal values represent what is motivational to you. They are cognitively and emotionally important principles that guide your life.[1]

Generally speaking, the more your day-to-day behaviors align with and support your values, the stronger your quality of life. In other words, you can improve your quality of life by moving toward valued life goals.[2] Therefore, it can be helpful to periodically sit down and reflect on your daily behaviors and how you spend your time, and ask yourself if your behaviors match your values. If they don't, this can signal areas of possible helpful change. For example, if one of your values is interpersonal connection and you haven't talked with, or spent time with, a loved one in several weeks, this may signal an opportunity to create a goal related to your relationships, such as calling a friend twice a month. This is not meant to be a critical exercise where you judge or criticize yourself for not living your values, although these realizations may be painful. That pain is valid and you can practice radical acceptance of that pain. You are creating an opportunity for reflection and possible increased motivation for helpful change. We tend to feel more motivated and interested in making a change if it is meaningful and important to us, and living in a way that supports our values enhances vitality and a sense of meaning.

Also, there is no right or wrong when it comes to values. Values are not based on what you think you should find important or meaningful, based on what others think, or what sounds good on paper. Values are about what you find personally meaningful. They are subjective. For example, you do not need to value "fitness" just because it sounds good and it seems like something you should value. Maybe you don't care about fitness and instead value learning. That's totally fine. Again, there is no right or wrong. Also, if you find your behaviors don't match your values, and you decide it would be helpful to make some changes, aim to create small and realistic goals that are achievable and offer the opportunity to enhance your quality of life. When creating goals, it is often best to start small and add to goals over time as helpful. Relatedly, if you have multiple goals, you don't need to do them all at once. Prioritize your goals by asking yourself, "What is most important to me, or most helpful to me, right now?" The aim is to start taking action that moves you toward your values, not necessarily choosing the right or best goal. If your goals are values-based, you can't really make a poor choice.

Values

Values are what you find meaningful in life. They are what you care about and consider important. Values are different for everybody, and they can change over time.

Values are different from goals. Goals can be achieved, whereas values are more like compass directions that you want to head in. For example, you might have the goal of calling a friend while placing value on your relationships.

You may not spend much time thinking about your values. When you feel stressed or down, have a decreased sense of purpose, or are uncertain about life, thinking about what is important to you and what makes life meaningful is helpful. Gaining clarity of your current values sets you up to take action that moves you toward your values.

Below is a list of values. Take a few minutes to circle the ones that are most important to you, and feel free to add other value words that are important to you and not listed.

honor	learning	curiosity	boldness
wisdom	flexibility	structure	loyalty
integrity	reliability	kindness	fitness
peace	order	calm	excitement
beauty	respect	helpfulness	wit
family	thoughtfulness	wonder	open-mindedness
generosity	patience	humor	self-sufficiency
adaptability	tolerance	organization	independence
faith	serenity	resilience	interdependence

spirituality	attentiveness	support	security
love	equality	meaning	belonging
strength	caring	understanding	gratitude
communication	intimacy	intelligence	dependability
stability	adventure	simplicity	trust
self-expression	play	risk	imagination
fun	courage	spontaneity	creativity
gratitude	leadership	comfort	productivity
drive	forgiveness	intuition	willingness
affection	warmth	compassion	health
connection	discipline	diversity	perseverance
joy	justice	experience	freedom

In your journal, record the answers to the following questions:

- From the values you circled above, what are your top five values?
- What do these values mean to you?
- How do you personally define them?
- How does your behavior reflect your values? Do your daily behaviors align with your larger values?

If your daily behaviors do not align with your values, use "Helpful Goals Are SMART" in chapter 5 to create goals that align your daily behaviors with your values. Example: You value relationships, yet you have not talked with your friends in a few weeks. In this example, your daily behavior does not align with your value. So, to live your life in a more meaningful and value-based way, you could set a goal related to calling a friend. For example, I will call John on the third Sunday of every month.

Remember, this exercise is not meant to be critical: "I am not doing a good job; I should do better." Rather, it is meant to remind you of what is most important to you. By thinking about your values, you can create more intentional choice in your behaviors, and by setting and implementing realistic goals that align your behaviors with your values, you can feel more motivation, meaning, and purpose in life.

It is natural to struggle with unpleasant parts of our experience, such as pain, fatigue, and anxiety, and this struggle, or tug-of-war, can keep us from moving in the direction of our values because we are using our time and energy to struggle. Once you clarify your values, the aim is to take your pain, fatigue, anxiety, or whatever you may be resisting with you as you move in the direction of your values. Practicing the skills in this book will help you shift from struggling to taking values-based action. You can also use the metaphor of putting whatever you don't like in a backpack and carrying it with you as you move toward your values. The backpack may be heavy, and you may want to put it down, yet it doesn't have to overtake you. Let it be there and carry it with you as you move toward what is meaningful to you.

The Choice Point

One of my favorite acceptance and commitment therapy (ACT) skills, developed by Dr. Russ Harris and colleagues, is called the choice point.[3] Viktor Frankl, the Austrian psychiatrist and Holocaust survivor, allegedly said, "Between stimulus and response there is a space. In that space is our power to choose our response. In our response lies our growth and our freedom."[4] The space Frankl is referring to can feel fleeting and elusive, and if you practice slowing down, noticing your experience in the moment, and intentionally considering how you want to respond, you can make more helpful decisions and engage in behaviors that are aligned with your values.

When practicing slowing down and cultivating the space between stimulus and response, it is useful to utilize the framework of the choice point. The choice point is the space you are in right before making a decision. It's a moment where you can pause and connect with your why before you decide on how to respond. You can visualize the choice point as a fork in the road—one road is your "towards" moves, and one road is your "away" moves. Your towards moves are the actions and decisions you make that move you in the direction of your values, and your away moves are actions and decisions that distance you from your values. Using the choice point framework is a useful way to remind yourself of the benefit of making towards moves, and how the small values-based choices you make each day add up and get you closer to your larger values. You can implement the choice point framework in a series of steps:

1. **Pause before acting or making a decision.** Ask yourself what you are thinking and feeling in the moment and give yourself space to make an intentional decision that aligns with your values.

2. **Connect with your why—your values.** What is important to you in life? What do you want to stand for in life? What qualities do you want to bring to your actions? Considering these types of questions can help you act in a way that aligns with your values. For example, one of my values is relationships, and two qualities I aim to bring to relationships are patience and caring. When I am tired and feeling irritable and talk to my loved ones in a sharp tone of voice, I am not acting in a way that aligns with my larger values. If I can stop and remind myself of this in the moment, it helps me pause, take a breath, and speak more calmly and caringly.

3. **Make your towards moves.** Once you have clarity on how you are feeling in the moment and your values, practice making your towards moves. Sometimes, these moves may be clear and straightforward, like in my example of speaking in a more caring tone of voice. At other times, and when making a big, more complicated decision, it might not be very clear. One way you can clarify your towards moves is by writing out different ways you can move forward and circle the towards moves while crossing out the away moves. As you do this, ask yourself what action or decision moves you in the direction of your values. If there are multiple choices, you can make a pros and cons list to determine what may be most helpful in the moment or what action you want to start with.

The bottom line: You have the power to choose, and your choices have power.

Tuning in to the present moment, slowing down or pausing, being grateful for the finite and incredible life I have, being balanced and flexible in my thinking and perspective, reminding myself what brings me joy, and spending time cultivating that joy and my other values is a work in progress. Some days I practice helpful skills more than others, and that is okay. I can confidently say that I am more self-accepting and self-compassionate now than in the past, and accepting myself and connecting to the joy I feel in the moment help set the stage for living my values as I am not using time and energy struggling with my thoughts, feelings, or physical sensations.

I continuously work to accept my internal experiences and have developed a more holistic and integrated sense of personal identity that encompasses the various facets of my personality and experience, including my disability. Sure, at times, I may still feel a brief pang of surprise when I catch a glimpse of my reflection when walking down the street, or feel a twinge of embarrassment when I fall in public, and I am ultimately not embarrassed by my disability or by myself. I don't live in a vacuum. I care what people think of me, and I care more about what I think of myself. I am proud of the actions I take to live my values and proud of myself and all my multifaceted humanness.

CHAPTER SEVEN

Harness Empathy for Post-Traumatic Growth

IF A MAGICAL BEING appeared in front of me and told me they could take away my cerebral palsy, I don't think I would take them up on their offer. My CP has benefitted me even with the challenges it can bring. For example, it has allowed me to be more aware, empathic, understanding, determined, persistent, grateful, and courageous, even if I didn't initially want to be. It is possible I would have these traits without CP, and it makes sense to me that my CP has enhanced, if not created, these traits. I value them, and they are a part of my sense of identity. So, taking away my CP, particularly earlier in my life, would be taking away a part of me that shapes who I am.

I also value cultivating a flexible, broad, and empathic perspective, being able to look outside my own viewpoint to understand someone else's viewpoint. I don't need CP to be empathic and flexible in my thinking, yet I think my CP facilitated, and perhaps sped up, my ability to appreciate the hardships others experience. Further, as a person with a disability, I am part of a large minority group and understand that those in minority groups often don't have the rights, privileges, and access that others do. For example, when I am not easily able to access a building, I am acutely aware of my disadvantage and how the world is not set up to meet my needs. This sends a message that society does not view me as important or as having the same value as an able-bodied person. As disheartening and frustrating as this is, I am glad I have a personal understanding of systemic inequalities and how crucial it is to continue to fight for and make progress toward disability justice.

I have an interesting relationship with snow. It can create a beautiful, magical, and cozy winter wonderland. It feels relaxing to snuggle up inside with a mug of tea as snow is falling outside. Snow also hinders my mobility and makes it more challenging to get around. One winter in Salt Lake City, so much snow had fallen while I was at work that by the time I arrived home in the evening, and parked in the building's uncovered parking lot, I had to literally crawl to my back door because the ground was too slippery to walk on. I don't always have to crawl to get around, and even a mild storm can be a huge obstacle. I cannot navigate icy, snowy sidewalks well. Even a seemingly small mound of snow at the curb in a crosswalk can make it nearly impossible to cross the street.

While not all of us have had the experience of abruptly losing mobility, most of us have had some type of experience that is emotionally challenging and painful and which can highlight how easy it may be to lose our abilities and privileges. Because of this sense of loss and shifting identity, it can be easier for us to empathize with people in situations different from our own.

Self-Reflection Exercise: Empathy

I encourage you to take some time to think about these questions about empathy and write out your responses in your journal.

- Have you ever been in a situation where you temporarily or permanently lost an ability or privilege? If so, how did you feel toward yourself? Toward other people?

- What does empathy mean to you?

- Do you consider yourself to be an empathic person? If so, why? If not, why not?

- When have you felt deep empathy? What about this situation enabled you to feel empathy?

- When do you not feel empathy? What are the barriers to empathy for you?

- What makes an interpersonal interaction/conversation meaningful to you?

- When do you feel most present and tuned in to other people? What gets in the way of you paying attention to others?

- What are some of your most important values? How do these relate to empathy?

- Who is the most empathic person you know? What do you value about this person?

What Is Empathy?

Empathy, the ability to imagine and understand the perspective of another person,[1] is a beneficial trait to cultivate. It is natural to be focused on your own perspective, thoughts, and feelings and to be closed off from the perspectives of others, particularly when they differ from your own. Nonetheless, empathy supports understanding, connection, and satisfying relationships, and it boosts self-esteem and pride.[2] Empathy can also increase self-awareness as you may come to more fully understand yourself by aiming to understand others. Empathy can be practiced and developed. Below are some ways you can do so:

- Be curious, ask questions, and listen to the answers. Open-ended questions that cannot be answered with a simple yes or no are helpful.

- Focus on listening not talking when having conversations. Use nonverbal cues such as eye contact and nodding your head to show the other person you are listening.

- Expose yourself to differences. For example, consume diverse media, go to new places, or visit a community you've never spent time in.

- Pay attention and practice being fully present. Limit distractions.

- Read or watch character-driven stories. Relating to others, including through books, shows, and movies, can help to understand others' experiences.

- Be willing to learn. You don't have to agree with someone else's perspective to understand it. Focus on learning about others' experiences.

- Find similarities, not differences. Commonalities can help foster empathy. Maybe the person you are talking to likes the same type of food or music you do. Or perhaps you are both parents.

- Be mindful of making assumptions, jumping to conclusions, or mind reading. Slow down and internally acknowledge that you don't know what another person is thinking and may not know the reasons why something is happening. In other words, what you are thinking may be inaccurate.

- Practice self-compassion. Practicing being compassionate with yourself can help facilitate empathy because a part of self-compassion is connecting to common humanity and understanding that all people have difficult moments and struggles. Recognizing shared experiences may make it easier to understand another person's perspective.

While my CP has facilitated, or strengthened, helpful aspects of my personality, I hold a sense of loss and sadness related to not knowing what it is like to have a more physically capable body. I get tearful thinking about how I will never know what it feels like to do seemingly simple physical movements like easily kneeling down on the floor or fluidly walking up or down a set of stairs. This is a loss, and it is natural to feel sad. Sadness is not bad, although we often think it is, and doesn't need to go away. Emotions are messengers, and it is helpful to pay attention to what they are telling you. They help drive your actions and alert others to your needs. Sadness, for example, can be a signal to take time to care for yourself following a loss. Or it can signal to others that you may want some comfort.

In broad terms, grief is the experience of distress associated with loss, and research has shown that having empathy, or the ability to take on another person's point of view, can lessen the intensity of grief. It has been proposed that shifting your focus from yourself to another person's perspective and needs enhances motivation to be helpful to the person and lowers distress. Further, adopting another person's perspective requires cognitive distancing from your own perspective, which may help you process grief in a less emotionally overwhelmed manner.[3] Grief is a universal experience, and research has shown that people tend to have more empathy for others who they relate to or who come from a similar background.[4] Through this lens, grief may facilitate empathy because it is a common experience that we can relate to.

Post-Traumatic Growth

Living with a chronic health condition or disability can significantly impact a person's life. It can alter a person's activities, daily roles, future plans, and physical and mental health. Research has demonstrated that the degree of distress someone experiences related to chronic health conditions varies and that factors such as social support and a sense of overall emotional stability can influence the degree of distress.[5]

Personal growth can come from loss, distress, and challenge. This is encapsulated in the psychological concept of post-traumatic growth (PTG). Post-traumatic growth is defined as the subjective experience of positive psychological change, or transformation, due to experiencing a highly stressful event.[6] Living with a chronic health condition or disability is not necessarily traumatic and may not be experienced as highly stressful, yet it can be challenging and cause distress. Understanding the concept of PTG is useful in recognizing that distress can facilitate change and personal growth.

Experiencing growth does not decrease or take away distress. It is not a way to feel better, be positive, or try to force yourself to find a silver lining in hardship. On the contrary, ongoing distress is often necessary for growth. Also, not all pain has a meaning or a larger purpose. Sometimes it just is. PTG is simply an understanding and recognition that loss and challenge may transform us in beneficial ways. Examples of PTG include an increased appreciation of life, setting new life priorities, feeling a sense of increased personal strength, identifying new possibilities, improving the closeness of relationships, and effecting positive spiritual change.[7]

It is important to acknowledge and honor your experience as it is, and not assume growth will occur or think something is wrong with you if you do not experience some type of growth after a highly stressful experience. It might even seem to invalidate the difficulties you have faced to consider that growth has occurred. It might not. Nonetheless, it is worthwhile to understand the possibility of PTG. It is human nature to think in all-or-nothing terms, to think something is all bad or all good. Yet, this is often not the case. Life is a mixed bag. Experiencing growth does not mean you are pleased that hardship happened. It simply means that hardship can lead to a variety of outcomes. For example, perhaps you have experienced loss and distress related to a professional role and have also deepened a friendship or decided to prioritize your value of creativity by pursuing creative activities that you have historically put off.

During or after challenging experiences, it can be helpful to give yourself time to reflect on your experiences and connect with supportive people. More specifically it may be beneficial to

+ Carve out time to explore your thoughts and feelings about your experiences. This may involve talking with supportive friends, writing or journaling, or engaging in an activity that allows you to connect with your emotions such as art or listening to or playing music.

+ Reflect on the meaning of the challenge within the context of your life. For example, how has the situation changed how you view yourself or your life priorities?

+ Consider how the hardship possibly challenged, or changed, your beliefs. Hardship often challenges the beliefs and assumptions we have about the world. This can be a difficult process as we may be forced to think about ourselves and the world in a new way. This process may also create more flexible thinking and growth.

+ Reflect on your strengths.

+ Connect with, and communicate with, others.

+ Use emotional coping skills such as observing your internal experience, practicing mindfulness exercises, practicing self-compassion, doing breathing exercises, and engaging in physical movement.

Part 3

CARING
FOR
YOUR
BODY

CHAPTER EIGHT

Connect with Your Body

WHEN MY PAIN OR tightness increases, or when I start each morning in pain, I can find myself saying, "My body is broken." To me, this is a shorthand way of acknowledging my pain and discomfort. It can be difficult to keep how I am feeling physically from leading me to become mentally stuck or separating my physical pain from my behaviors. For example, I may be experiencing pain, yet it is not helpful to repeatedly tell myself how miserable I feel on a never-ending loop in my mind or talk to my partner in an irritated tone of voice. And focusing on how my "body is broken" is inaccurate and does not acknowledge the completeness of my body as it is. Disabled bodies are not broken, even when it feels like they are.

My family used to go to Hilton Head Island, South Carolina, for an annual beach vacation. One of my favorite things to do there was ride an adult tricycle down the long, flat beach. Riding that trike gave me a rare sense of physical freedom. It was fun and not too challenging. I didn't have much pain, and it felt like I could ride forever with the wind in my face. Joy! Freedom! A part of me also felt sad each time I would ride because it was a reminder that I don't feel physical freedom and ease often. It is unusual for me to feel physically unencumbered, and I can think my body is a burden. That is tough. And it is important to remember that thoughts are not facts. I can think my body is a burden at times and that does not mean it is a burden.

When I was younger, I did not feel appreciative of my body. My body represented difference, discomfort, and inability. It was the thing that separated me from my friends, caused me to be unable to do things I wanted to do, and made it harder to get through the day. I saw the "brokenness," not the ability and wonder. I wasn't thinking about how my organs were functioning properly or that I had more mobility than a lot of people. I was focused on what I thought was wrong and what I wished was different. I wanted to be able-bodied, not "broken." I wanted to have more physical flexibility and balance. I wanted to take a dance or group exercise class without having to make modifications. I wanted to be able to wear more types of shoes.

Self-Reflection Exercise: How You Relate to Your Body

I encourage you to take some time to think about these questions about how you relate to your body and write out your responses in your journal.

+ What thoughts do you have about your body?

+ What emotions arise when you think about your body?

+ How does your body physically feel day-to-day? Do you experience any consistent physical sensations?

+ On a scale of 0 to 10, with 0 being not at all and 10 being extremely, how satisfied are you with your body?

+ When have you felt most satisfied with your body? What factors contributed to you feeling this way?

+ When have you felt least satisfied with your body? What factors contributed to you feeling this way?

+ In general, what makes you feel comfortable in your body?

+ If you experience chronic pain, on a scale of 0 to 10, with 0 being none and 10 being extreme pain, what is your average daily pain level?

+ What makes your pain worse? What makes your pain better?

+ If you experience chronic fatigue, on a scale of 0 to 10, with 0 being none and 10 being extreme fatigue, what is your average daily fatigue level?

+ What makes your fatigue worse? What makes your fatigue better?

The human body is wild and complex. It is amazing that my lungs are bringing oxygen into my body and removing carbon dioxide and that every minute my heart is beating about a hundred times and sending blood and nutrients all over my body. As I have mentioned, constant fatigue and pain are the biggest physical challenges of my CP, and it is important to acknowledge how I am feeling in any given moment while also remembering that I am more than a body and that my body is not broken. Also, it is beneficial to be intentional about how I behave and aim to behave in a manner that is helpful and values-based. One way I enable myself to be more intentional and not allow my emotional distress, physical pain, or fatigue to dictate my behavior is by practicing relaxation exercises.

Physical pain and emotional stress often go hand-in-hand. When we are stressed, our muscles tense, as increased muscle activation is one of the physiological responses to cognitive stress,[1] and stress and muscle tension trigger pain. Chronic stress, limited ability to habituate to or manage stress, or a prolonged physiological reaction to stress are factors in chronic pain. Also, physical pain can cause stress, as those with pain tend to report higher levels of emotional distress compared to those without pain, which in turn can increase muscle tension and create more pain.[2] Therefore, one helpful way to manage stress and chronic pain is to practice relaxing your muscles and nervous system via relaxation exercises. You don't have to experience chronic pain to benefit from relaxation exercises: These exercises are useful for managing the stress and anxiety of daily life that pretty much all of us experience.

Many beneficial relaxation exercises exist, and I am going to outline some of my favorites. While it is true that there are times when it is helpful to engage in longer relaxation exercises—if your muscles are particularly tense or your emotional intensity is high, it may take fifteen to twenty minutes to feel a sense of relaxation. I am a fan of practicing brief exercises that you can realistically implement. Brief practice may mean taking a few intentional deep breaths throughout your day or sitting and breathing for several minutes.

One quick way to practice relaxation exercises is to pause multiple times per day, perhaps three times a day, or once an hour, and take about three to five intentional breaths using one of the breathing styles from the exercises below. Of course, you can practice for longer if you like. And it is important not to wait until emotional or physical stress or pain increases to practice these exercises. They will be most effective if you practice them when you are not super stressed or in a lot of pain. This will help you to remember to use them and will make them more effective when your stress or pain increases.

Simple Breathing Exercises

1. Breathe slowly and rhythmically: Practice breathing slowly in and out. Imagine your breath is a wave in the ocean that is slowly coming ashore, and then slowly receding back into the ocean. See if you can practice breathing in this slow and steady fashion for two to five minutes, or longer if that's helpful.

2. Breathe through your nose. It can be helpful to practice breathing from your nose only. This helps you to breathe more slowly, which can aid stress relief. So, practice keeping your mouth closed and breathing in and out from your nose. Again, practice breathing slowly.

3. Lengthen the exhale portion of your breath. The exhale part of the breath is the most relaxing. The exhale is like a brake for your nervous system helping it slow down. Practice making the exhale portion of the breath about twice as long as the inhale. For example, if you naturally inhale to a count of three, practice slowly exhaling to a count of five or six.

   Interestingly, the opposite type of breath, where you lengthen the inhale portion, can be helpful when you are feeling tired and want to activate your nervous system rather than slow it down. To practice this type of breath, inhale slowly to a count of five or six, and exhale to a count of three, or whatever count comes naturally to you.

Belly Breathing Exercise

Breathe from your belly. Diaphragmatic or belly breathing is the most physiologically relaxing type of breath. When you breathe using your belly, you stimulate the vagus nerve, which activates the relaxation response, reducing your heart rate and blood pressure and lowering stress.[3] With belly breathing, you want to breathe deeply into your belly.

To practice this, sit or lie down, placing one hand on your chest and the other hand on your belly. Slowly inhale through your nose, practicing keeping the hand on your chest still, and allowing the movement to come from your belly. When you inhale, your belly should rise as if you have a balloon in your belly that is filling with air, and when you slowly exhale, your belly should gently collapse as if the balloon is deflating.

If you are not familiar with belly breathing, it can take practice. To help yourself become familiar with how belly breathing feels, sit or lie down in a comfortable and relaxed position with your arms and legs uncrossed.

Place one hand on your belly at the waistline and the other hand on the center of your chest. Start by becoming aware of your breathing. Without trying to change anything, simply notice how you are breathing. Notice where you are breathing from: whether your shoulders are rising and falling, whether your chest is rising and falling, or perhaps your belly is rising and falling. Notice how your hands move as you breathe.

Now notice the rate of your breathing. Are you breathing rapidly or slowly? Are you breathing deeply or shallower?

Now as you slowly inhale, imagine the air flowing deeper into your belly. Feel your belly fill with air, as if it is a balloon, as your lower hand rises. Briefly pause at the top of your breath, and then slowly breathe out as you completely exhale, letting the balloon deflate. Slowly take a breath in: 1, 2, 3, 4, and slowly exhale: 1, 2, 3, 4. Let any tension melt away as you relax more deeply with each exhale.

Notice how the air feels, as cool air enters your nose, passes through your nose, and flows into your lungs. Notice the movement of your breath as you slowly breathe in and out. Feel the temperature of each breath, cool as you inhale and warm as you exhale. It may be helpful to count your breaths as you breathe in and out: inhale 1, exhale 1, inhale 2, exhale 2 . . .

Notice your breath becoming smooth and slow. Feel your belly expand outward with each inhale and then gently collapse with each exhale. Feel yourself become more relaxed with each exhale. Allow your shoulders to become heavier with each exhale. Continue breathing slowly, gently, and deeply. Breathe deeply into your belly.

As you breathe, continue to notice the movement of your breath, and the cool temperature of the air, as it enters your nose. Notice how the air becomes warmer as you follow it deep into your belly and out through your nose or mouth.

Continue breathing slowly, gently, and deeply. Breathe deeply into your belly. Let any tension melt away as you relax more deeply with each exhale.

Progressive Muscle Relaxation

Progressive muscle relaxation (PMR) is a relaxation exercise where you go through the major muscle groups of the body intentionally tensing your muscles and then releasing them. Practice tensing each muscle group for about five seconds before releasing. Doing this allows you to bring more intentional awareness to how a tense muscle feels versus a relaxed muscle and can make it easier over time to relax your muscles. If tensing your muscles exacerbates pain, practice tensing your muscles more gently, or feel free to skip this exercise.

Begin by sitting in a chair or lying on a couch. Take a few slow breaths and allow your body to sink into the chair or couch.

First, build up the tension in your hands and lower arms by making tight fists with your hands and pulling your fists up by bending your wrists. Feel the tension through your fingers, knuckles, hands, wrists, and lower arms. Focus on the sensation of tension and hold this tension for a few seconds.

Now release the tension. Let your hands and lower arms relax onto the chair or couch beside you. Focus your attention on the relaxed sensations in your hands and arms. Feel the release from tension as you relax your muscles fully. Take a couple of slow breaths.

Now build up the tension in your upper arms by pulling your arms back and in toward your sides. Or curl your arms as if you are doing a bicep curl. Feel the tension in your arms, shoulders, and into your back. Focus on the sensation of tension. Hold this tension for a few seconds.

Now release your arms and let them relax, almost feeling heavy at your sides. Notice the difference between the prior sensations of tension and the new sensations of relaxation. Your arms might feel heavy, warm, and relaxed. Take a couple of slow breaths.

Now bring your attention to your feet and lower legs. Build up the tension by flexing your feet and pulling your toes toward your upper body. Feel the tension as it spreads through your feet, ankles, shins, and calves. Hold this tension for a few seconds. Now, release all the tension in your feet and lower legs. Let your feet and leg muscles relax. Feel the difference in these muscles as they relax. Feel the release from tension, the sense of comfort, the heaviness of relaxation. Take a couple of slow breaths.

Build up the tension in your upper legs and buttocks by pressing your knees together and lifting your legs slightly off the ground or couch. Focus on the sensation of tightness through your legs and buttocks. Hold this tension. Now release all the tension, letting your legs sink heavily into the chair or couch. Let all the tension fully release as your legs sink farther into the chair or couch. Focus on the feeling of relaxation and comfort. Take a couple of slow breaths.

Build up the tension in your abdomen by pulling your abdomen in toward your spine, very tightly. Feel the tightness and focus on this tension, holding it for a few seconds. Now let the tension in your abdomen relax. Take a couple of slow breaths, allowing your breath to be smooth and slow. Feel the comfort of relaxation.

Build up the tension in your chest by taking in a deep breath and holding it. Feel the tension. Now slowly let the air escape and resume normal breathing, letting air flow in and out slowly, smoothly, and easily. Feel the difference in sensations as the muscles relax, compared to tension.

Build up the tension in your neck and shoulders by pulling your shoulder blades back and up toward your ears. Feel the tension around your shoulders, neck, and upper back. Hold this tension. Now release the tension. Let your shoulders drop down, sinking farther until they are completely relaxed. Notice the difference between the previous sensations of tension and the new sensations of relaxation. Take a couple of slow breaths.

Build up the tension in your mouth, jaw, and throat by opening your mouth as wide as it will go and holding it open. Feel the tightness. Now release the tension. Let your mouth close and the muscles around your throat and jaw relax. Notice the difference between the sensations of tension and the sensations of relaxation. Take a couple of slow breaths.

Now build up the tension around your eyes and lower forehead by squeezing your eyes tightly shut. Hold this tension. Now release all the tension in your eyes and lower forehead. Let the tension melt from around your eyes. Feel your forehead and eyes smooth. Feel the difference as the muscles relax. Take a couple of slow breaths.

Build up the tension in your upper forehead and scalp by raising your eyebrows as high as possible. Feel the wrinkling and pulling across your forehead and the top of your head. Hold this tension. Now release all the tension in your forehead, letting your eyebrows relax. Focus on the sensations of relaxation. Take a couple of slow breaths.

Your whole body is feeling relaxed and calm. Scan your body for any remaining tension, and if you notice any, continue breathing slowly and gently, letting the tension go with each exhale. Spend a few minutes in this relaxed state noticing your breathing. Feel the cool air as you breathe in and the warm air as you breathe out. Allow your breathing to be smooth and slow. You are feeling comfortable and relaxed.

Cultivating a Sense of Agency

Another way I cope with my physical limitations is by intentionally cultivating a sense of agency in my body. A sense of agency refers to the notion that you have control over your actions, of making something happen.[4] There are a lot of things in life that we have no, or little, control over, and it is helpful to develop agency over the things we can control. In other words, take action to strengthen the belief that you can engage in a certain action and it will likely have a certain outcome. For me, it is beneficial to specifically cultivate agency in my body, in the belief that my body is capable, even when it doesn't feel capable, and remembering that it does a lot of seemingly ordinary, yet extraordinary, things every day.

One of the main ways I develop and enhance agency is through physical movement. For a long time, I have prioritized regular physical movement. There are many physical and mental benefits of physical movement, including decreasing depression and anxiety and increasing socialization and participation in life activities.[5] One reason I enjoy it is because it reminds me of what my body can do and allows me to have an empowered experience with my body even if I am tight or sore. Physical movement also connects me to the present-moment felt experience of my body versus being focused on thoughts about my body. When I am moving, I am often focusing on how my body is feeling in the moment versus what I think about my body. In other words, it allows me to have a mindful experience and connect to the here and now. Recently, I had moderate symptoms of COVID-19 for about two weeks and did not move much. Once I felt better and started moving my body again, I had a clear sense of coming back to my body. I felt more connected, more whole, more myself.

Another reason I prioritize physical movement is that it helps me manage my chronic pain and fatigue. When comparing active adults to more sedentary peers, research suggests there is an association between physical activity and reduced feelings of low energy and fatigue.[6] A study with individuals with fibromyalgia or chronic fatigue syndrome showed that participants got into a cycle where pain and fatigue led to inactivity, and inactivity led to more pain and fatigue.[7] Of course, physical activity can worsen pain and fatigue and it is important to pace activity and rest. Research has also shown that a range of physical movements, including low-intensity daily activities, movement therapies such as tai chi and yoga, and higher-intensity movement can help chronic pain.[8] In general, my pain and fatigue are worse when I don't move my body. For example, I exercise in the mornings before work, and on days I do not exercise, my body is stiffer and my fatigue is worse throughout the day, and in particular in the mornings. The increased energy I feel due to exercise typically does not last more than a few hours, yet the boost is noticeable. It is as if someone charged my battery for longer, and I have a bit more pep in my step.

Physical movement exists on a wide continuum, and I encourage you to define movement broadly depending on your specific needs. For some, movement may mean going for a jog or a brisk walk. For others, it may mean stretching or gently moving their arms and legs as they sit in a chair. If you define movement too rigidly, it can limit you and potentially hinder developing agency in your body. Physical movement does not need to be defined as running a marathon. Low-intensity movement, walking at a casual pace, can be just as helpful at boosting energy as higher-intensity movement.[9]

Increasing Physical Movement

Below are some general tips for increasing physical movement. Hold these ideas loosely, as they may not fit everyone. Also, not everyone has the privilege of mobility, and it is important to acknowledge that moving is an option for many of us, but not all. For the purposes of this chapter, I am focusing on the power of physical movement to increase your sense of agency and assurance in your body, what it is capable of, and to manage pain and fatigue, which in turn supports your overall well-being.

- ◆ Start small and go slow. You do not need to move for a long time or move with speed or intensity to feel the benefits of movement. Start with five or ten minutes. Engaging in low-impact or low-intensity movement such as stretching, walking, swimming, yoga, Pilates, light dance, or biking may be helpful as these types of movements can be easier on the joints and muscles and more doable for people with limited mobility or chronic health conditions while also improving quality of life.[10]

Here are some examples of low-intensity physical movements.

- Make small movements with your arms or slowly kick your legs back and forth while sitting.

- Sit in a chair, hold the sides of the chair, and with your knees bent, slowly march your legs up and down: lift your left leg, place it down, then lift your right leg, and so on.

- Stretch while seated in a chair or on the ground. For example, while seated, you can cross your arms over your chest with your hands resting on your shoulders, and while keeping your hips still, gently twist your upper body to the left and then to the right.

- Lift light weights while seated or standing. For example, you could do seated bicep curls with three-pound weights.

- Walk or bike at a casual pace.

If you want to, you can add time or intensity as you go. Yet, this is not a requirement. You get to engage in movement however you want to.

- If able to walk, strive to walk more. Consider your current daily routine and see if there are ways you can slowly, and realistically, increase the amount you walk. Perhaps this means scheduling a once-a-week walk with a friend or taking a gentle stroll with your dog.

- Move more at home. This may look like cleaning, gardening, yard work, or stopping every thirty to sixty minutes if you're sitting (set an alarm on your phone) and stretching, doing some shoulder rolls, or walking around the room.

- Create a more active lifestyle. This may mean exploring new enjoyable physical activities that appeal to you. For example, taking an exercise class, going on a hike, joining a walking group, or dancing around the house to music. Take breaks throughout the day to gently move and stretch your body, or create a move goal. For example, "I will move my body for thirty minutes three days a week, on Mondays, Wednesdays, and Fridays, by going for a walk outside or doing a yoga video at home." Refer to "Helpful Goals Are SMART" in chapter 5 for guidance on creating goals.

◆   Make movement fun. Physical movement does not need to be a chore. Movement can be whatever you want it to be. What sounds fun to you? Walking, dancing, stretching, hiking, swimming—there are a lot of options! Activities may need to be adapted to meet your mobility needs. For example, a gentle water aerobics class may be more doable than swimming, or look online for accessible hiking trails in your area. Also, consider taking time to explore the world through your hands or body versus through your thoughts. This may mean coloring, playing with clay, making some type of art, or playing a musical instrument.

◆   Make movement social. A lot of people enjoy movement more if it involves socializing. Consider engaging in a physical activity with a friend or joining an exercise group or class. If taking an exercise class, it may be helpful to ask about accessibility, including if the instructor has experience working with a range of mobility needs, and you may need to advocate for modifications. I would encourage you to speak up if a certain movement does not work for your body and ask for an alternative.

CHAPTER NINE

Tolerate Discomfort and Acknowledge the Complexity of Your Experience

PEOPLE STARE AT ME all the time. Typically, it doesn't bother me. It bothers my partner more if he's with me because he feels uneasy with attention. One day, after being stared at a lot when walking around town, we joked that I should get a T-shirt made that says, "It's called cerebral fucking palsy." It can be unsettling to be stared at whenever you leave the house. I am sure a lot of people can relate to this—being outwardly different in some way and people not knowing how to react to you or reacting poorly or inappropriately. A person may not intend anything negative when staring, and yet the act of being stared at can make us feel as though we are under a microscope. It creates that sense of, "What? Is something wrong?"

I am a bad dancer and I like to dance. I have not let being bad stop me from dancing. A few years ago, I was getting my groove on at a wedding and having fun. At a breakfast for the married couple the next morning, a wedding guest came up to me and started diagnosing my disability, critiquing my dancing, and offering me unsolicited recommendations for how I should move my body. He explained that he worked in the medical profession and knew the ins and outs of my disability. He then suggested that I should move my arms and feet more to make my dancing smoother and more rhythmic. I was dumbstruck that the conversation was happening. I said something about enjoying dancing and not really caring what I look like on the dance floor. Then, I tried to end the conversation as quickly as possible and move on with my morning. However, I did not move on from the conversation in my head. I couldn't believe this man thought he had the right to talk to me about my disability in this way.

I have noticed that disabled people are not treated with the same level of bodily autonomy and privacy as able-bodied people. It's as if we don't get control and sovereignty over our bodies, and others have the right to invade our space or offer advice without permission. For example, strangers have attempted to hug me as I am walking down the street, which is completely unnerving and potentially dangerous. No, you do not get to touch me without my consent because I am disabled.

It is natural to notice novelty and I don't begrudge others for staring, which is different than touching. I understand that if I have a strong reaction to someone staring at me, it is related to my own perception or projection. The times that I react strongly to being stared at are the times I am feeling more insecure in my body. When I was younger, I had a stronger reaction to being stared at because, to me, it highlighted my difference and made me feel inferior. It felt as if being stared at somehow made my CP more severe or more noticeable when what I wanted was to blend in. Part of my work and growth related to self-acceptance has been to more fully come to terms with the fact that my CP is noticeable, and that is okay.

Society tells us that being disabled, or different, is bad, ugly, wrong, and inferior. It takes time and intentional self-work to unlearn these messages. The interesting thing is that if we are lucky enough to live long lives, all of us will likely experience some form of physical limitation or disability at some point in our lives. Yet, something being universal, at least at some point in one's life, does not make it any less scary or anxiety-provoking. Humans tend to not like change. We like to feel a sense of stability, coherence, and internal equilibrium, and disruption to our sense of coherence can cause distress.[1] Yet, distress often leads to growth.[2] If you are not uncomfortable, at least at times, life can feel stagnant and ultimately not as meaningful. Personal growth and self-acceptance involve more fully accepting and appreciating the complexity of your experiences. I can feel insecure at times and go out into the world with my head held high. I can lack confidence in my abilities and show up in my life each day. I can feel a bit uneasy if someone is staring at me and have empathy for looking at something novel because I do it too.

Self-Reflection Exercise: Tolerating Discomfort

I encourage you to take some time to think about these questions about tolerating discomfort and write out your responses in your journal.

- What emotions do you consider unhelpful or negative? What emotions do you consider helpful or positive?

- Is it uncomfortable for you to experience emotions you consider negative? If so, what is uncomfortable about it? Are these emotions associated with certain unpleasant thoughts or physical sensations?

- On a scale of 0 to 10, with 0 being not at all and 10 being extremely, how uncomfortable is it for you to experience negative emotions?

- Do you experience certain emotions strongly? If so, which ones?

- On a scale of 0 to 10, with 0 being not at all and 10 being extremely, how much do you avoid experiencing negative emotions?

- If you try to avoid negative emotions, how do you do so?

- When feeling upset or negative emotions, do you try to do something immediately to make the emotions go away? If so, what do you do?

- On a scale of 0 to 10, with 0 being not at all and 10 being extremely, how difficult is it for you to have emotions without trying to do something to change them?

Tolerating Emotional and Physical Discomfort

It is common to want to avoid unpleasant or uncomfortable feelings and physical sensations, to think of uncomfortable emotions or sensations in a negative way, or to try to make them go away. For example, if I am feeling embarrassed, I might think, *I hate feeling this way.* Or, if I am feeling anxious, or in physical pain, I might think, *This feels awful. I need it to go away.* Your level of tolerance toward discomfort is based on how much unease you feel about it, how unbearable it seems, and how much you want to get rid of it. While it is true that you can problem-solve and get rid of some external factors and physical sensations—if you are cold, you can put on a sweater; if it is raining and you don't want to get wet, you can use an umbrella—when you try to apply this same problem-solving or get-rid-of approach to your internal experience, it often makes things worse.

The more you struggle with or avoid your emotions, distress, or physical sensations, the more intense they get. When emotions are acknowledged, expressed, and thought about in a more helpful and balanced way, "Anxiety isn't good or bad, it just is; I can cope with this," you set the stage for increasing your self-awareness, finding social support, and using helpful coping skills. When emotions are avoided, they are reexperienced with heightened physiological arousal, which can increase physical sensations such as chronic pain. For example, research with people with fibromyalgia showed that suppressing or avoiding emotions was related to more severe pain.[3]

Emotions and physical sensations, even unpleasant ones, are messengers. They are signals that provide you with information, including information about what you care about. Generally speaking, if you are upset about something, you care about it or something it is related to. If you didn't care, you wouldn't feel upset. Also, emotions and physical sensations are not permanent (at least not completely permanent; even those of us with chronic pain experience fluctuating levels of pain intensity). They are changing experiences that vary and eventually pass. An emotion or sensation passing does not necessarily mean it completely goes away. Passing could mean the intensity decreases, or that we are less focused on it, or feel less held back by it. When I practice allowing my emotional and physical experience, let it be, let it "hang out," it passes quicker than if I struggle against it. For example, if my fatigue is more intense at the end of the day, and I ruminate about it and repeatedly tell myself how horrible it is, it feels stronger. If I practice taking a few slow breaths and making room for the fatigue, it is less consuming and usually not as strong. This is helpful to me for many reasons, including that it ultimately saves me emotional and physical energy because I am not using energy fighting what is. Here are some additional suggestions for how you can practice tolerating emotional and physical discomfort.

Practice observing your experience. See if you can practice watching or observing your experience as if you can stand to the side of yourself and nonjudgmentally notice what is happening. It might be helpful to think of a documentary filmmaker who is holding a camera and filming what is in front of them. This person is not judging what is happening; they are simply filming it. It is important to remind yourself that no matter what you are experiencing, you are not your thoughts, emotions, or physical sensations. You are an observer of your experience and bigger than any piece of your experience.

Name your experience. As mentioned earlier, it is helpful to practice naming your experience in a curious and nonjudgmental way. You can practice this by completing the following sentences: "I am having the thought that . . ." "I am feeling . . ." "I am having the physical sensation of . . ." "I am having the urge to . . ."

Use imagery. In chapter 4, I talked about the skill of cognitive defusion and creating mental space from your thoughts and how you can practice this skill by using imagery, such as imagining your thoughts as a wave that moves in and out from the shore, clouds that pass in the sky, or credits that move up a movie screen. You also can visualize your thoughts as moving through a room with an open front and back door. You can use these same images with your emotions and physical sensations, practicing letting them come and go without pushing them away.

Focus on the present moment. Once you have observed and named your experience, allowing it to come and go, practice focusing your attention on the present moment. This could be focusing on a task that is in front of you, or a sight, sound, smell, taste, or texture. Or you may focus on your breath and the sensation of your breath moving in and out of your body.

Allow emotions and physical sensations to come back. Emotions and physical sensations come and go. They are not permanent, yet they tend to fluctuate in intensity and circle back around again like a suitcase on a luggage carousel that goes round and round many times. This is okay. When this happens, go back to observing them and letting them come and go at their own pace.

And, Not But

This leads me to another one of my favorite ACT skills, using the word *and* instead of *but* when you talk to yourself and others. This is called the "Kick Your Buts" or "Get Off Your Buts" exercise.[4] We frequently use the word *but* in everyday conversation.

"I want to call my friend, but I am tired."

"I'm sorry I verbally snapped at you, but you were being defensive."

"I was planning to go for a short walk, but my legs are sore."

"I would go to the party, but I am feeling too anxious."

But can seem innocuous, and when we use it, we naturally focus on whatever follows the *but* and tend to ignore the first part of our experience. *But* can discount, exclude, dismiss, negate, or cancel what precedes it. In the example, "I want to call my friend, but I am too tired," it is common to focus on being tired and negate the desire to connect with a friend. Intentionally using the word *and* allows for complexity and dichotomy in your experience. *And* acknowledges, includes, and expands what precedes it.

Multiple things, even contradictory things, can occur at the same time. If I say, "I want to call my friend, and I am tired," I am acknowledging that both are happening. I can be tired *and* choose to call my friend. *And* allows for behavioral options and psychological flexibility. If you practice acknowledging all aspects of your experience, you can make a more intentional choice about how you want to act versus focusing on only one aspect of your experience and acting out of habit or comfort. *And* enables you to decrease cognitive rigidity and more fully embrace the complexity of your experience, and decreasing cognitive rigidity is associated with psychological flexibility and increased psychological well-being.[5] You can be sad and joyful at the same time, for example. You don't have to choose or narrowly focus on certain aspects of your experience. Using the word *and* instead of *but* is a skill. It is something that can be practiced and strengthened. A skill that can increase your ability to notice and accept your full experience. So, I encourage you to "Get off your buts" and use *and* instead.

CHAPTER TEN

Give Yourself Permission to Do Things Differently

I DON'T RECALL A MORNING in my life when I woke up feeling energized. I have had mornings where I feel less tired, not rested or energized. I consistently feel as though I am running on about a quarter tank of gas, trying to move through the tasks of daily life as though my tank is full. It feels like someone strapped a bunch of weights to my body, filled my brain with fuzz, and sent me on my way. At least a few times a day, I think about how tired I am and how much better I would likely feel if I had more energy. I would be unstoppable! The reality is that I don't have a lot of energy, and I have had to practice embracing this reality and giving myself permission to engage in daily life in a way that supports my well-being.

Giving Yourself Permission

We all tend to move through the world in certain ways. Some of us may be "human doers" versus human beings, constantly pushing to complete task after task. Some of us may be naturally talkative or quiet. Some of us may tend toward solitude, while others may love to be around people. There is no right or wrong, no good or bad way to be. However, we often hold certain beliefs about the correct or "right" way to do something or move through the world, and we tend to stick with behaviors we are comfortable with. These habitual behaviors may not be the most helpful. At least, they may not be helpful all the time.

It can be challenging to give yourself permission to do something differently, to challenge your automatic, and often unhelpful, thoughts and behaviorally push yourself out of your comfort zone. Often, before you can practice other helpful coping skills and behaviors, you need to first give yourself permission to try a different approach, even if it feels uncomfortable. This also can be challenging because we are typically used to asking others for permission to do things rather than granting ourselves permission, particularly in childhood when we asked our parents for permission to go out with friends or spend money.

This tendency to ask others for permission, or to wait to do something until someone else gives us permission, can remain with us in adulthood and can strengthen unhelpful patterns of behavior and decrease our sense of self-trust, self-confidence, and self-empowerment. Giving yourself permission takes practice, and there are often numerous opportunities to practice each day, such as giving yourself permission to ask for help when it's needed or giving yourself permission to rest when feeling tired.

One way to give yourself permission is to make a permission list. To do this, write a list of behaviors you would do, or do more regularly, if you gave yourself permission. Then slowly start to practice the behaviors on your list. If you are having difficulty thinking of examples, consider behaviors that you are currently doing that are unhelpful and then consider what a more helpful, or opposite, behavior may be.

Another way to consider possible helpful ways to give yourself permission is to focus on "want to" versus "have to." For example, maybe you are telling yourself, "I have to work on this task for two more hours," yet if you consider your "I want to," you think, "I want to go for a walk outside." Practice doing your "want to" versus telling yourself you must continue your "have to."

Reframing Rest

A lot of us struggle to slow down and rest, to feel okay with rest. Someone does not need to be coping with chronic fatigue or chronic pain to give themselves permission to rest. We live in a society that values productivity and output, a society that tells us we are lazy if we rest and that *lazy* is a bad word. Rest has been defined as interrupting physical, mental, or emotional activity, a temporary break from work, or a sense of peace, tranquility, or serenity.[1] Humans are not robots; we all have finite amounts of energy, and we must stop to refill our tanks and replenish ourselves so that we can continue to do the things that are meaningful to us. I intentionally remind myself of the importance of rest and give myself permission to rest. I remind myself that I am not doing anything "bad" or "wrong" by resting. Quite the opposite; I am recharging my batteries and supporting my well-being so that I can more effectively engage in the activities that are valuable and important to me.

While I remind myself of the importance of rest, I am also a fairly anxious person and a "doer," which can make it challenging to stop and rest. I don't like the feeling of a task being incomplete and hanging over my head. When confronted with a task I am not expecting, or thinking about my to-do list, I can feel overwhelmed in the moment, and I want to immediately jump in and get things done. It is hard for me to sit and let something be, even if I know it is not an urgent task. This tendency is related to my natural temperament and is also amplified by my fatigue. I tell myself that my energy is limited and that it's better to get something done now and not have to think about it than to do it later. I get a reinforcing burst of temporary relief when a task is completed; however this approach has costs. The to-do list of life is never-ending, and if I am constantly pushing to get things done and get them done now, my fatigue is worse. I am not fully allowing myself to rest and recharge. That is why I have had to practice being aware of my behavioral tendencies, natural rhythms, and limits. For example, I have more energy and perform tasks more effectively in the morning or daytime versus in the evenings. And I practice tolerating the discomfort of sitting with the anxiety that arises when doing things differently.

In other words, not jumping to complete a task as soon as possible creates anxiety, and it has taken time to learn via my direct experience that it is truly okay not to work on a task immediately. I'm continuing to learn that it is okay to let something sit and not respond right away. We have all learned to think and do things a certain way through messages we have received over time from others as well as interactions with the environment. This is called behavioral reinforcement. If you get rewarded for a certain behavior via praise, which is positive reinforcement, or your anxiety goes down after doing a behavior, negative reinforcement, it is likely the behavior will continue.[2] This learning is often ingrained, yet it is possible to unlearn unhelpful patterns and relearn more helpful ones.

To do this, you need to be intentional and deliberate about your behaviors versus operating on automatic pilot, and be aware of thoughts that may lead to certain behaviors so you can reframe these thoughts as needed. By practicing not immediately responding to tasks, at least not all the time, I have taught myself that if a task is important, it will get addressed at some point. I don't have to chase it down. I don't have to do it right now. I can focus my time and energy on what is most helpful to me in the moment, which is often taking a break and focusing on my values of joy, well-being, connection, and relationships.

Pacing Yourself

In our go-go-go world, pacing, along with resting, may seem like a dirty word. The skill of pacing is often used when managing chronic pain, yet it can be helpful to all of us. Pacing is a behavioral approach that allows for engaging in a moderate level of consistent activity rather than over-pushing and then over-resting.[3] The idea here is that people are prone to "pushing through," whether that is pushing through pain, tiredness, or stress, to complete a task and not stopping until the task is complete. This overactivity, or pushing through at all costs, is then followed by needing long amounts of time to physically and mentally recover (underactivity). The back and forth between over- and underactivity can lead to increased stress and anxiety, decreased efficiency, lowered self-esteem, and avoidance of activity. Engaging in a moderate level of activity and proactively resting is how you stop this unhelpful over-under cycle. The skill of pacing uses time as the guide for activity engagement. Pacing is about balancing activity level, planning ahead, and working "smarter not harder."

How to Pace

1. Before you begin an activity or task, estimate the amount of time you can engage in the activity without having a flare-up in pain, fatigue, stress, or something else that might cause you distress.

2. Set that time, minus about one to five minutes (we tend to overestimate how long we can do something), as your "active" goal time for the activity.

3. Now, estimate the amount of resting time you need to resume the activity without or with less pain, fatigue, or stress, or to continue with your day. This is your "rest" time.

4. Each active goal time plus rest time equals one cycle. For example, if the activity you need to complete is a work presentation, you may estimate that you can work on it for two hours without an increase in stress, and then you need to rest for fifteen minutes. So, working for two hours and resting for fifteen minutes is one cycle of pacing.

You may engage in multiple cycles of activity and rest or just one cycle, depending on the task and how you are feeling. Your estimated active and rest times may need to be adjusted as you go and gather information based on your direct experience. Aim to stick with pacing regardless of whether you are having a "good" or "bad" day to not get stuck in an over-activity-underactivity cycle. For example, on days you feel less pain and fatigue, you may want to throw pacing out the window and keep going, which can lead to feeling more pain and fatigue later. Moderation is the key. Remember to be realistic and set doable goals. Spread out activities. If your pain or fatigue flares up, feel free to stop even if you have not met your active goal. You can always add more activity time later, as needed, and as your mental and physical abilities and stress levels allow.

Self-Reflection Exercise: Awareness of Your Tendencies

I encourage you to take some time to think about these questions about your behavioral and emotional tendencies and write out your responses in your journal.

- Are you someone who tries to complete tasks as soon as possible, or someone who tends to push tasks off?

- Do you typically move through tasks quickly, or do you tend to take a fair amount of time?

- What emotions arise for you when you are confronted with a to-do list—stress, anxiety, calm, boredom?

- Relatedly, what emotions arise for you when tasks are uncompleted, particularly uncompleted for a fair amount of time?

- Is it difficult for you to rest or take a break when tasks are uncompleted?

- In general, what are your personal expectations related to completing tasks? Do you desire tasks to be completed in a particular way?

- Do you notice yourself using words or phrases such as "perfect" or "not good enough"? Is it difficult for you to feel satisfied with how you complete a task?

- Do your expectations vary depending on the type of task, or are they consistent?

- What emotions or thoughts arise when you do not meet your expectations?

- What are the benefits and costs of your automatic behaviors and tendencies? Understanding the benefits and costs of your current behaviors can help to highlight what you may want to do differently.

Emotions influence behaviors. For example, if feeling anxious about a task, you may jump to complete it quickly, or you may push it off to avoid anxiety. As mentioned earlier, it is common to want to make emotions, particularly unpleasant ones, go away. When you are feeling anxious, your chest may feel tight, your stomach may feel uneasy, or you may be mentally caught in worry. These sensations are uncomfortable, so you automatically have the urge to make them go away. Yet, jumping to try to improve or fix your emotional experience can backfire and fuel emotional intensity. So, while it may feel unnatural or uncomfortable, it is helpful to practice making room for emotions and tolerating discomfort, knowing that doing so can feel unpleasant yet is not harmful.

Once you are aware of your behavioral tendencies, you can consider what you may want to do differently. It can be helpful to keep in mind that even if a behavior seems ultimately unhelpful, it serves a function, and you are getting some type of benefit out of it, or else you would likely not do it. For example, my behavior of jumping to complete tasks as soon as possible serves the function of easing anxiety. If a task is complete, I don't have to think or worry about it, which saves me energy in the long run, or so I tell myself. I encourage you to reflect on your tendencies with compassion rather than with judgment or criticism. The aim is to reflect on tendencies matter-of-factly and curiously. You are recognizing that a behavior is unhelpful in a specific context, not necessarily unilaterally, and choosing to do something differently in the moment without labeling yourself as bad.

If you never practice doing anything differently, you never have the opportunity to challenge rigid thoughts that you must behave in a certain way. By practicing doing something differently, you are creating a type of behavioral experiment where you can practice something new and see what happens, versus predicting the outcome before you start. Think of this as collecting data. For example, was your fatigue better, worse, or the same when you practiced not completing tasks as quickly as possible? Did the day feel any differently? Did you feel more distress, anxiety, or joy?

You may hesitate to do something differently because you believe there will be a poor outcome or you won't be able to cope if things don't go smoothly. This is a form of making a prediction, of assuming you know what is going to happen before you do something. You don't know what is going to happen. Even if things have gone poorly in the past, that does not mean, or guarantee, things will go poorly in the future. Yes, you can't assume things are going to go well, just like you can't assume things will go poorly. You just don't know. Not knowing can feel scary. It also can feel freeing. It opens the door to possibility, of trying a behavior and seeing what happens. By practicing doing something differently, you can enhance your self-confidence and teach yourself that you have robust abilities to cope, even when life is bumpy.

To change your behavior in helpful ways, it is important to build awareness of your tendencies and patterns, and practice tuning in to your internal experience (refer to "Tuning In to Internal Experience" in chapter 1). One of the main ways I care for myself is by practicing tuning in to how I am feeling in the moment, asking myself what I need, and knowing my limits so that I can implement helpful behaviors and boundaries. As I mentioned above, my automatic tendency is often to push, push, and push. This is not sustainable. It leaves me feeling more fatigued and more irritable. So, I strive to practice slowing down, tuning in to how I am feeling, not ignoring my emotions and physical sensations, saying "no" as needed, and giving myself permission to rest.

A beneficial outcome of tuning in to your internal experience is cultivating awareness of your stress signs and psychological and behavioral limits. Your stress signs are markers of your limits. Stress signs can be physical, emotional, and behavioral. For example, muscle tension, headache, stomach pain, irritability, helplessness, tearfulness, difficulty focusing, or difficulty making decisions are stress signs (a chart of "Common Stress Signs" is included later in this chapter). If I notice I am becoming more irritable and my physical pain is increasing in intensity, I am approaching my psychological or behavioral limit, and it would be helpful to shift my behavior in a way that decreases the intensity of my stress signs, for example, practicing slow, deep breathing.

Window of Tolerance

The window of tolerance is a concept developed by Dr. Dan Siegel to describe the optimal zone of arousal for a person to be in to function in daily life. When a person is within this window, they can effectively manage and cope with their emotions. Being within your window of tolerance includes feeling generally calm and alert, processing information effectively, and experiencing a range of emotions. When you are outside your window, you have less ability to cope with emotions. Stress, particularly high levels of stress, can cause you to be pushed out of your window of tolerance. And when you are pushed out, you may be in a state of heightened arousal and feel less control over your actions, or be in a state of hypoarousal and feel shut down or numb.[4]

Awareness of your emotional experience and stress signs is key to recognizing when you are pushing up against the limits of your window of tolerance or are outside your window of tolerance. Once you recognize these signs, you can take action to bring yourself back into your optimal window. Many coping skills, such as grounding exercises (refer to the "5-4-3-2-1 Grounding Technique" in the Introduction), slow deep breathing, reframing thoughts to be more balanced and neutral, and engaging in movement that feels soothing, are designed to help you stay in, or return to, your window of tolerance.

Window of Tolerance and Stress Signs

I encourage you to take some time to think about these questions about your window of tolerance and stress signs and write out your responses in your journal.

- ◆ How do you know when your window of tolerance and coping skills are being stretched to the maximum? In other words, what are your stress signs?

- ◆ How do you know when it would be helpful to stop and rest or do something differently? For example, do you notice yourself becoming more irritable?

- ◆ Do your thoughts change? For example, are you more critical of yourself or others?

+ Do you notice certain physical sensations in your body, such as increased muscle tension and soreness?

+ Do your behaviors change? If so, how? For example, do you talk in a frustrated tone of voice or act impatiently?

You may be skilled at ignoring your stress signs and continuing to push, push, push. You may be able to get away with this for a while, yet eventually, this approach will catch up to you. You may start to feel more consistently anxious or depressed. You may experience more physical health concerns, or your relationships may deteriorate. Therefore, it is beneficial to practice tuning in to your stress signs to have more opportunities to set limits, practice sticking to them, and engage in behaviors that support your well-being. Further, it is important not to wait until you are at your wit's end and your limits are stretched to the maximum to take care of yourself. In general, any coping skill, such as pausing and taking a few slow breaths, is going to be more effective if you practice it proactively. This helps to build familiarity with a skill and makes the skill more effective when stress increases. Below, you'll find a chart of "Common Stress Signs." I encourage you to consider if any of these signs apply to you and if there are additional signs that aren't listed that you notice yourself experiencing.

Once you notice your internal experience, the next helpful step is to practice letting your experience guide your action. You can do this by asking yourself, "What do I need right now?" or "What would be helpful to me right now?" Of course, the answer to this question can take many forms. A simple and effective action may be to pause and breathe for a moment or two and then proceed with your day. Or a larger shift in behavior may be helpful. And the most helpful action may be the action that does not come automatically or easily, or is the opposite of what you typically do.

Common Stress Signs

PHYSICAL	BEHAVIORAL	EMOTIONAL	COGNITIVE
headache	overbearing attitude	crying	trouble thinking clearly
stomachache	critical attitude	irritability	forgetfulness

PHYSICAL	BEHAVIORAL	EMOTIONAL	COGNITIVE
sleep difficulty	avoiding tasks, procrastination	nervousness or restlessness	decreased ability to focus
back pain	hyperfocus on tasks	boredom	constant worry
tight shoulders or neck	overusing substances	feeling powerless or helpless	thoughts of running away or escape
chest pain, racing heart	fidgeting	sense of pressure or overwhelm	inability to make decisions
tiredness, fatigue	low motivation, inability to do things	anger	fearful anticipation
dizziness	over- or undereating	loneliness	poor judgment

Opposite Action

One of the helpful techniques from dialectical behavior therapy (DBT) is opposite action, a skill where you choose to do the opposite of what your emotions are telling you to do—your emotional urge—particularly when your emotions want to lead you to engage in ineffective or detrimental behavior. Opposite action is intended to decrease unhelpful emotional urges and increase helpful emotions.[5] For example, perhaps you are feeling down and have the urge to stay in bed all day. Yet, you know that if you stay in bed too long you will feel worse. In this example, a helpful opposite action would be to choose to get up and engage in a small action (brush your teeth or change clothes), even if you don't feel like it. Or perhaps you are feeling sad and want to avoid others and isolate yourself. A helpful opposite action may be to text, call, or spend time with a loved one.

It is important to remember that emotions are not good or bad. Emotions are messengers. They are signals that can provide you with useful information. For example, anger may signal that a possible injustice has occurred, or anxiety may signal a possible threat. Yet your emotions do not always send you accurate and helpful information; the signal can misfire, and emotions can dictate your behaviors in unhelpful ways. Further, at times it can even feel like our brains and bodies are hijacked by strong emotions. The intensity of the emotion consumes us and we can't think clearly. So, it is important to practice slowing down and asking yourself questions, such as "What would be helpful to me right now?" A helpful behavior may be different than your emotional urge. It is also important to recognize that you can separate emotions from behaviors and practice acknowledging and honoring your feelings without judgment while choosing to engage in helpful behaviors. For example, you can acknowledge that you feel sad and make room for sadness while choosing to reach out to a friend instead of isolating yourself for a long time.

Below are a few examples of action urges associated with certain emotions and helpful opposite actions that can be practiced. This list is adapted from the book *DBT Training Skills Manual,* Second Edition by Marsha M. Linehan, PhD.[6]

EMOTION	ACTION URGE	OPPOSITE ACTION
fear or anxiety	escape or avoid	engage, don't avoid
anger	attack	step back; approach with kindness
sadness	withdraw or isolate	be active; connect with others
shame	hide or avoid	talk with others
inadequacy	self-criticism	self-compassion

Saying No

Most of us have a lot of practice saying "yes" to things, to taking on more and more. This can be related to a variety of factors, including people-pleasing, concern over the perceptions of others or fear of letting others down, and believing we need to prove our worth. It is not easy to say "no." And saying no can be beneficial. It is a way for you to honor and prioritize your needs and remind yourself, via your behaviors, that you are inherently worthy and you don't have to prove your worth. Saying "no" is a skill. It can feel uncomfortable initially and often feels more familiar and comfortable over time.

For better or for worse (most often for the better), my CP and chronic fatigue frequently force me to slow down, be aware of my limits, and practice saying no to certain tasks and invitations. I only have so much energy each day, and the reality of not having as much energy as some other people do means I have to practice slowing down and, at times, doing less. I have learned that I need to nurture and protect my well-being. Others are not going to do it for me! One of the ways I do less is by saying no. I jokingly like to say that I am socially a bit "lame," meaning I am often content being at home and I don't like to routinely engage in social activities that take a lot of effort and planning. It can feel self-affirming to say no if doing so allows you to be authentic, aligns with your genuine desires and values, and supports your well-being. And that does not mean saying no is easy. Nonetheless, it is a skill that you can strengthen over time.

Here are some tips for practicing saying no:

Be aware of your priorities and values. Identify what is important to you and what is not. If you don't know how you want to spend your time, it can be challenging to know how you do not want to spend it. Before you can practice saying no, you need to be aware of what you want to say no to. It is helpful to write out a list of your priorities and values, and you can use the "Values" list in chapter 6 to help with this.

Separate the request from the person. You can say no and be kind and appreciative. You can thank someone for thinking of you and extending an invitation, or making a request, and still say no. You may think saying no means you are being disrespectful or mean. This isn't true. It is possible to communicate directly and respectfully. Separate the request from the person. You are saying no to the request, not the person. You are not rejecting a person by saying no to a request.

Practice. Saying no is often challenging and requires practice. Practice saying no out loud to yourself or saying no in less anxiety-provoking situations, such as saying no to someone offering you something to eat that you don't like. Also, practice saying no without apologizing. You haven't done anything wrong by saying no.

Give people a heads up. If you know in advance that there are certain requests or situations you plan to say no to, it can be helpful to let others know ahead of time. For example, I do not like engaging in social activities on Friday evenings as I am tired from the week, so I might say to a friend, "Hey, just so you know, I don't typically like to do things on Friday evenings as I tend to be particularly tired at that time, so please know that I may say no to requests to go out on Fridays."

Repeat yourself as needed. Some people may circle back and ask again even if you have said no. Don't be afraid to be firm and repeat yourself. Again, you can be firm, direct, and respectful.

It is okay to miss out. You may hesitate to say no because you are fearful of missing out. That's understandable, and remember that when you practice saying no to something, you are also saying yes to your priorities and values. You may be focusing on what you are missing, and it can be helpful to remind yourself what you are gaining by saying no.

Embrace vulnerability. Again, saying no isn't easy for a lot of people. It can make you feel vulnerable as you may worry about letting someone down or someone thinking about you critically. Remember that embracing vulnerability allows you to honor yourself and helps you build courage. Courage isn't about not feeling anxious or uneasy. It is about feeling these emotions and acting anyway.

Afterword

Perfectly Imperfect: It's an Ongoing Journey

CHANGING OUR RELATIONSHIP WITH our thoughts and practicing helpful coping skills and behaviors are not easy. Cultivating self-acceptance, managing mood, and leaning into emotional vulnerability and self-growth, for example, are long-term nonlinear processes. I can confidently say I have more self-acceptance and self-compassion today versus fifteen or twenty years ago, and I regularly catch myself saying critical things about myself. I also tend to act reactively and irritably when my tiredness or pain increases. So, while I practice the coping skills in this book, I am a nonperfect human who is on an ongoing journey toward increased self-acceptance and living my personal values.

While it is true that there are many things in life we cannot control, and many barriers that we must overcome, it is also true that how we relate to our thoughts and feelings and the behaviors we choose to engage in can have a big impact on our daily lives and quality of life. The skills presented in this book aim to help you get cognitively, emotionally, or behaviorally unstuck and increase your psychological flexibility: your ability to create mental space from unhelpful thoughts or create more helpful thoughts, connect to the present moment, acknowledge and allow your thoughts, emotions, and physical sensations without feeling consumed or controlled by them, and engage in values-based behavior even when it feels challenging to do so.

The skills throughout this book not only increase psychological flexibility but also a sense of empowerment. They allow you to feel more confident and capable of controlling the factors that you can, and to respond to your internal experience in a helpful and meaningful way whether you can change it or not. They can enhance your sense of self-acceptance, self-confidence, and self-worth, decrease anxiety and other mood symptoms such as depression, and aid you in feeling more empowered in your body and life.

Some goals are concrete and specific. You can complete them and be done. I wrote this book with the hope that it will help readers enhance a sense of tenacity, courage, and self-acceptance. These are values, not goals. While you can create specific and helpful goals related to them, moving toward the larger values is an ongoing process that often cannot be fully completed. We don't get to a point where we feel 100 percent self-acceptance, for example.

Nonetheless, every day I witness people using the evidence-based coping skills in this book to make progress toward their goals and live their values. So, I hope the coping skills in this book help you move toward both your goals and values. I hope you feel more capable and empowered to control what you can control, set and achieve helpful goals, live your personal values, and enhance your well-being and quality of life. I also hope my personal experiences as a disabled woman are a reminder of our shared humanness and how we all can experience low self-worth or feelings of anxiety or depression, for example, and offer an encouragement that you too can practice the skills in this book to feel more confidence, courage, and self-acceptance.

As I mentioned in the Introduction, remember that learning any type of new skill, and developing the ability to implement it effectively, requires practice, patience, and repetition. Be compassionate with yourself. It is okay to start small. It may be initially helpful to pick just one coping skill in this book to implement. And if you stop practicing the skills, that is okay too. You can always start again. Each new moment is an opportunity to start again or keep going. You are capable.

Here's to us and to the ongoing journey of cultivating tenacity, courage, and self-acceptance. Cheers!

Acknowledgments

I COULD NOT HAVE WRITTEN this book without the support, encouragement, and guidance of many people, and it is with much gratitude that I express my appreciation to these individuals. To my husband, Sean, for his unwavering support, encouragement, and love throughout the entire writing process. You patiently listened to me talk about this book nonstop, and your belief in me was an incredible motivator. Thank you for everything. To my parents and family for their unconditional love and support and for always believing that I can accomplish anything I set my mind to. Receiving that type of love and support is not a given, and I know how fortunate I am. To my friends who provided me with encouragement, and a dose of fun, whenever needed. I want to especially acknowledge my friend Sarah Campbell, who was the first person, and only friend or family member, to read a draft of this book before it was published. Sarah, your valuable feedback and belief in me and this book helped it exist. Thank you. To my colleagues who provide a warm and supportive work environment and challenge me to consistently learn and grow. To my clients throughout the years who have taught me so much about courage and the capacity for change and growth. It is a privilege to be a part of your journeys. And to the team at North Atlantic Books. Your skill, thoughtfulness, and guidance have been invaluable. Thank you for making my dream come true.

Writing this book, and having it be in the world, has been a dream of mine that has been years in the making, and I could not have achieved this incredibly meaningful accomplishment without the support and love of those around me. Thank-you does not encompass all the gratitude I feel, and thank you, nonetheless.

Notes

Introduction

1. Karen Gasper and Cinnamon L. Danube, "The Scope of Our Affective Influences: When and How Naturally Occurring Positive, Negative, and Neutral Affects Alter Judgment," *Personality and Social Psychology Bulletin* 42, no. 3 (2016): 385–99, https://doi.org/10.1177/0146167216629131.
2. Amy Thornhill Pakula, Kim Van Naarden Braun, and Marshalyn Yeargin-Allsopp, "Cerebral Palsy: Classification and Epidemiology," *Physical Medicine and Rehabilitation Clinics* 20, no. 3 (2009): 425–52, https://doi.org/10.1016/j.pmr.2009.06.001.

Chapter 1: Learn Emotion Regulation Skills

1. Amelia Aldao and Andre J. Plate, "Coping and Emotion Regulation," in *Process-Based CBT: The Science and Core Clinical Competencies of Cognitive Behavioral Therapy*, ed. S. C. Hayes and S. G. Hofmann (Oakland, CA: New Harbinger, 2018), 261–72.
2. Magdalena Kozubal, Anna Szuster, and Adrianna Wielgopolan, "Emotional Regulation Strategies in Daily Life: The Intensity of Emotions and Regulation Choice," *Frontiers in Psychology* 14 (August 13, 2023): 1218694, https://doi.org/10.3389/fpsyg.2023.1218694.
3. James J. Gross and Oliver P. John, "Individual Differences in Two Emotion Regulation Processes: Implications for Affect, Relationships, and Well-Being," *Journal of Personality and Social Psychology* 85, no. 2 (2003): 348–62, https://doi.org/10.1037/0022-3514.85.2.348.
4. Katherine L. Dixon-Gordon, Amelia Aldao, and Andres De Los Reyes, "Emotion Regulation in Context: Examining the Spontaneous Use of Strategies Across Emotional Intensity and Type of Emotion," *Personality and Individual Differences* 86 (2015): 271–76, https://doi.org/10.1016/j.paid.2015.06.011.
5. Lise Solberg Nes, Shawna L. Ehlers, Mary O. Whipple, and Ann Vincent, "Self-Regulatory Fatigue in Chronic Multisymptom Illnesses: Scale Development, Fatigue, and Self-Control," *Journal of Pain Research* 2013 (6): 181–88, https://doi.org/10.2147/JPR.S40014.

6. Benjamin G. Shapero, Lyn Y. Abramson, and Lauren B. Alloy, "Emotional Reactivity and Internalizing Symptoms: Moderating Role of Emotion Regulation," *Cognitive Therapy and Research* 40 (2016): 328–40, https://doi.org/10.1007/s10608-015-9722-4.

7. Kayleigh Pleas and Cory Muscara, "The Practice of Mindfulness," in *Becoming Mindful: Integrating Mindfulness into Your Psychiatric Practice,* eds. Erin Zerbo, Alan Schlechter, Seema Desai, and Petros Levounis (Washington, DC: American Psychiatric Association, 2016), 25.

8. Marshall B. Rosenberg and Deepak Chopra, *Nonviolent Communication: A Language of Life* (Encinitas, CA: PuddleDancer Press, 2015); The Hoffman Institute Foundation, "Feelings List," 2013, www.hoffmaninstitute.org/wp-content/uploads/Practices-FeelingsSensations.pdf.

9. A. H. Maslow, "A Theory of Human Motivation," *Psychological Review* 50, no. 4 (1943): 370–96, https://doi.org/10.1037/h0054346, https://psychclassics.yorku.ca/Maslow/motivation.htm.

10. Cynthia J. Price and Carole Hooven, "Interoceptive Awareness Skills for Emotion Regulation: Theory and Approach of Mindful Awareness in Body-Oriented Therapy (MABT)," *Frontiers in Psychology* 9 (May 27, 2018): 335233, https://doi.org/10.3389/fpsyg.2018.00798.

11. Shelley E. Taylor, Baldwin M. Way, and Teresa E. Seeman, "Early Adversity and Adult Health Outcomes," *Development and Psychopathology* 23, no. 3 (2011): 939–54, https://doi.org/10.1017/S0954579411000411.

12. Natalie A. Masento, Mark Golightly, David T. Field, Laurie T. Butler, and Carien M. van Reekum, "Effects of Hydration Status on Cognitive Performance and Mood," *British Journal of Nutrition* 111, no. 10 (2014): 1841–52, https://doi.org/10.1017/S0007114513004455.

13. Nils Kohn, T. Toygar, C. Weidenfeld, M. Berthold-Losleben, N. Chechko, S. Orfanos, S. Vocke, et al., "In a Sweet Mood? Effects of Experimental Modulation of Blood Glucose Levels on Mood-Induction During fMRI," *Neuroimage* 113 (2015): 246–56, https://doi.org/10.1016/j.neuroimage.2015.03.024.

14. Gerald L. Clore and Jeffrey R. Huntsinger, "How Emotions Inform Judgment and Regulate Thought," *Trends in Cognitive Sciences* 11, no. 9 (2007): 393–99, https://doi.org/10.1016/j.tics.2007.08.005.

15. Steven C. Hayes, Jason B. Luoma, Frank W. Bond, Akihiko Masuda, and Jason Lillis, "Acceptance and Commitment Therapy: Model, Processes and Outcomes," *Behaviour Research and Therapy* 44, no. 1 (2006): 1–25, https://doi.org/10.1016/j.brat.2005.06.006.

16. Russ Harris, *ACT Made Simple: An Easy-to-Read Primer on Acceptance and Commitment Therapy* (Oakland, CA: New Harbinger, 2019).

17. Benjamin G. Feldman, "How Do Mindfulness Practitioners Describe Pausing?: A Qualitative Interview Study," *Bridgewater State University Undergraduate*

Review 14 (2018): 41–54, https://vc.bridgew.edu/cgi/viewcontent.cgi?article =1437&context=undergrad_rev.

18. Natalia E. Morone, Cheryl P. Lynch, Vincent J. Losasso, Karl Liebe, and Carol M. Greco, "Mindfulness to Reduce Psychosocial Stress," *Mindfulness* 3 (2012): 22–29, https://doi.org/10.1007/s12671-011-0076-z.

19. Joy Yeonjoo Lee, Adam Szulewski, John Q. Young, Jeroen Donkers, Halszka Jarodzka, and Jeroen J. G. van Merriënboer, "The Medical Pause: Importance, Processes and Training," *Medical Education* 55, no. 10 (2021): 1152–60, https:// doi.org/10.1111/medu.14529.

Chapter 2: Cultivate Unconditional Self-Compassion, Self-Acceptance, and Self-Worth

1. Hillary L. McBride, *The Wisdom of Your Body: Finding Healing, Wholeness, and Connection Through Embodied Living* (Ada, MI: Brazos Press, 2021).

2. Mia L. Pellizzer and Tracey D. Wade, "Developing a Definition of Body Neutrality and Strategies for an Intervention," *Body Image* 46 (2023): 434–42, https://doi.org /10.1016/j.bodyim.2023.07.006.

3. Veya Seekis and Rebecca K. Lawrence, "How Exposure to Body Neutrality Content on TikTok Affects Young Women's Body Image and Mood," *Body Image* 47 (2023): 101629, https://doi.org/10.1016/j.bodyim.2023.101629.

4. Windy Dryden, "Unconditional Self-Acceptance and Self-Compassion," in *The Strength of Self-Acceptance: Theory, Practice and Research,* ed. Michael E. Bernard (New York: Springer, 2013), 107–20, https://doi.org/10.1007/978-1-4614 -6806-6_7.

5. Kristin D. Neff, "The Development and Validation of a Scale to Measure Self-Compassion," *Self and Identity* 2, no. 3 (2003): 223–50, https://doi.org/10.1080 /15298860390209035.

6. Mark R. Leary, Eleanor B. Tate, Claire E. Adams, Ashley Batts Allen, and Jessica Hancock, "Self-Compassion and Reactions to Unpleasant Self-Relevant Events: The Implications of Treating Oneself Kindly," *Journal of Personality and Social Psychology* 92, no. 5 (2007): 887, https://doi.org/10.1037/0022-3514.92.5.887.

7. Christopher K. Germer and Kristin D. Neff, "Self-Compassion in Clinical Practice," *Journal of Clinical Psychology* 69, no. 8 (2013): 856–67, https://doi.org/10.1002 /jclp.22021.

8. Tim Desmond, *Self-Compassion in Psychotherapy: Mindfulness Based Practices for Healing and Transformation* (New York: W. W. Norton, 2016).

9. Tiffany A. Ito, Jeff T. Larsen, N. Kyle Smith, and John T. Cacioppo, "Negative Information Weighs More Heavily on the Brain: The Negativity Bias in Evaluative Categorizations," *Journal of Personality and Social Psychology* 75, no. 4 (1998): 887, https://doi.org/10.1037//0022-3514.75.4.887.

10. Alex M. Wood, Jeffrey J. Froh, and Adam W. A. Geraghty, "Gratitude and Well-Being: A Review and Theoretical Integration," *Clinical Psychology Review* 30, no. 7 (2010): 890–905, https://doi.org/10.1016/j.cpr.2010.03.005.

11. Robert A. Emmons, *Thanks!: How the New Science of Gratitude Can Make You Happier* (Boston: Houghton Mifflin Harcourt, 2007).

12. Rini Lestari and Maharani Fajar, "Gratitude, Self-Esteem and Optimism in People with Physical Disabilities," *Prizren Social Science Journal* 4, no. 2 (2020): 14–21, https://doi.org/10.32936/pssj.v4i2.150.

13. Charles S. Carver and Michael F. Scheier, "Dispositional Optimism," *Trends in Cognitive Sciences* 18, no. 6 (2014): 293–99, https://doi.org/10.1016%2Fj.tics.2014.02.003.

14. Lestari and Fajar, "Gratitude, Self-Esteem and Optimism."

15. Stanislava Popov, Jelena Radanović, and Mikloš Biro, "Unconditional Self-Acceptance and Mental Health in Ego-Provoking Experimental Context," *Suvremena Psihologija* 19, no. 1 (2016): 71–79, https://doi.org/10.21465/2016-SP-191-06.

16. Reinout E. de Vries, Jeroen Pronk, Tjeert Olthof, and Frits A. Goossens, "Getting Along and/or Getting Ahead: Differential HEXACO Personality Correlates of Likeability and Popularity Among Adolescents," *European Journal of Personality* 34, no. 2 (2020): 245–61, https://doi.org/10.1002/per.2243.

17. Paula R. Pietromonaco, Bert Uchino, and Christine Dunkel Schetter, "Close Relationship Processes and Health: Implications of Attachment Theory for Health and Disease," *Health Psychology* 32, no. 5 (2013): 499, https://doi.org/10.1037%2Fa0029349.

18. Alicia D. Cast and Peter J. Burke, "A Theory of Self-Esteem," *Social Forces* 80, no. 3 (2002): 1041–68, https://doi.org/10.1353/sof.2002.0003.

19. Albert Ellis, "Psychotherapy and the Value of a Human Being," in *Handbook of Rational-Emotive Therapy,* eds. Albert Ellis and Russell Grieger (New York: Springer, 1977), 99–112.

20. Catriona Mackenzie, Wendy Rogers, and Susan Dodds, "Introduction: What Is Vulnerability and Why Does It Matter for Moral Theory," in *Vulnerability: New Essays in Ethics and Feminist Philosophy* (New York: Oxford University Press, 2014), 1–29.

21. Doris Schroeder and Eugenijus Gefenas, "Vulnerability: Too Vague and Too Broad?" *Cambridge Quarterly of Healthcare Ethics* 18, no. 2 (2009): 113–21, https://doi.org/10.1017/S0963180109090203.

22. Marta Landoni, Milica Petrovic, Chiara Ionio, and Andrea Gaggioli, "Vulnerability and Informal Caregiver: A Scoping Review," *medRxiv* (2021), https://doi.org/10.1101/2021.09.02.21263030.

23. Deborah Lupton and John Tulloch, "'Life Would Be Pretty Dull Without Risk': Voluntary Risk-Taking and Its Pleasures," *Health, Risk & Society* 4, no. 2 (2002): 113–24, https://doi.org/10.1080/13698570220137015.

Chapter 3: Practice Radical Acceptance

1. Gerd Ahlström, "Experiences of Loss and Chronic Sorrow in Persons with Severe Chronic Illness," *Journal of Clinical Nursing* 16, no. 3a (2007): 76–83, https://doi.org/10.1111/j.1365-2702.2006.01580.x.

2. Sophie Lebel, Brittany Mutsaers, Christina Tomei, Caroline Séguin Leclair, Georden Jones, Danielle Petricone-Westwood, Nicole Rutkowski, et al., "Health Anxiety and Illness-Related Fears Across Diverse Chronic Illnesses: A Systematic Review on Conceptualization, Measurement, Prevalence, Course, and Correlates," *PloS One* 15, no. 7 (2020): e0234124, https://doi.org/10.1371/journal.pone.0234124.

3. Mark Freeston, Ashley Tiplady, Lauren Mawn, Gioia Bottesi, and Sarah Thwaites, "Towards a Model of Uncertainty Distress in the Context of Coronavirus (COVID-19)," *The Cognitive Behaviour Therapist* 13 (2020): e31, https://doi .org/10.1017%2FS1754470X2000029X; Ian A. Scott, Jenny A. Doust, Gerben B. Keijzers, and Katharine A. Wallis, "Coping with Uncertainty in Clinical Practice: A Narrative Review," *Medical Journal of Australia* 218, no. 9 (2023), https://doi.org/10.5694/mja2.51925.

4. Patrícia Pinheiro, Miguel M. Gonçalves, Daniela Nogueira, Rui Pereira, Isabel Basto, Daniela Alves, and João Salgado, "Emotional Processing During the Therapy for Complicated Grief," *Psychotherapy Research* 32, no. 5 (2022): 678–93, https://doi.org/10.1080/10503307.2021.1985183.

5. Marsha M. Linehan, *Building a Life Worth Living: A Memoir* (New York: Random House, 2021), 503.

6. Shaunna Siler, Tami Borneman, and Betty Ferrell, "Pain and Suffering," *Seminars in Oncology Nursing* 35, no. 3 (June 2019): 310–14, https://doi.org/10.1016/j .soncn.2019.04.013.

7. Noelia Bueno-Gómez, "Conceptualizing Suffering and Pain," *Philosophy, Ethics, and Humanities in Medicine* 12 (2017): 1–11, https://doi.org/10.1186/s13010 -017-0049-5.

8. James V. Cordova, "Acceptance in Behavior Therapy: Understanding the Process of Change," *The Behavior Analyst* 24 (2001): 213–26, https://doi.org/10.1007 %2FBF03392032.

9. Yara Mekawi, Sierra Carter, Grace Packard, Shimarith Wallace, Vasiliki Michopoulos, and Abigail Powers, "When (Passive) Acceptance Hurts: Race-Based Coping Moderates the Association Between Racial Discrimination and Mental Health Outcomes Among Black Americans," *Psychological Trauma: Theory, Research, Practice, and Policy* 14, no. 1 (2022): 38, https://doi.org/10.1037 /tra0001077.

10. John C. Williams and Steven Jay Lynn, "Acceptance: An Historical and Conceptual Review," *Imagination, Cognition and Personality* 30, no. 1 (2010): 5–56, https://doi.org/10.2190/IC.30.1.c.

Chapter 4: Change Your Relationship with Your Thoughts

1. Jeffrey C. Teal and Gary T. Athelstan, "Sexuality and Spinal Cord Injury: Some Psychosocial Considerations," *Archives of Physical Medicine and Rehabilitation* 56, no. 6 (1975): 264–68.

2. George Taleporos and Marita P. McCabe, "Body Image and Physical Disability—Personal Perspectives," *Social Science & Medicine* 54, no. 6 (2002): 971–80, https://doi.org/10.1016/S0277-9536(01)00069-7.

3. Peter M. ten Klooster, Lieke C. A. Christenhusz, Erik Taal, Frank Eggelmeijer, Jan-Maarten van Woerkom, and Johannes J. Rasker, "Feelings of Guilt and Shame in Patients with Rheumatoid Arthritis," *Clinical Rheumatology* 33 (2014): 903–10, https://doi.org/10.1007/s10067-014-2516-3.

4. Anne Werner, Lise Widding Isaksen, and Kirsti Malterud, "'I Am Not the Kind of Woman Who Complains of Everything': Illness Stories on Self and Shame in Women with Chronic Pain," *Social Science & Medicine* 59, no. 5 (2004): 1035–45, https://doi.org/10.1016/j.socscimed.2003.12.001.

5. Jeffrey Schwartz and Rebecca Gladding, *You Are Not Your Brain: The 4-Step Solution for Changing Bad Habits, Ending Unhealthy Thinking, and Taking Control of Your Life* (New York: Penguin, 2012).

6. Kristin N. Herzberg, Sean C. Sheppard, John P. Forsyth, Marcus Credé, Mitch Earleywine, and Georg H. Eifert, "The Believability of Anxious Feelings and Thoughts Questionnaire (BAFT): A Psychometric Evaluation of Cognitive Fusion in a Nonclinical and Highly Anxious Community Sample," *Psychological Assessment* 24, no. 4 (2012): 877–91, https://doi.org/10.1037/a0027782.

7. Deborah A. Roth, Winnie Eng, and Richard G. Heimberg, "Cognitive Behavior Therapy," in *Encyclopedia of Psychotherapy*, eds. Michel Hersen and William H. Sledge (Washington, DC: American Psychiatric Press, 2002), 451–58.

8. Odin Hjemdal, Tore Stiles, and Adrian Wells, "Automatic Thoughts and Meta-Cognition as Predictors of Depressive or Anxious Symptoms: A Prospective Study of Two Trajectories," *Scandinavian Journal of Psychology* 54, no. 2 (2013): 59–65, https://doi.org/10.1111/sjop.12010.

9. Tim Buschmann, Robert A. Horn, Virginia R. Blankenship, Y. Evie Garcia, and Kathy B. Bohan, "The Relationship Between Automatic Thoughts and Irrational Beliefs Predicting Anxiety and Depression," *Journal of Rational-Emotive & Cognitive-Behavior Therapy* 36 (2018): 137–62, https://doi.org/10.1007/s10942-017-0278-y.

10. Bas Verplanken, Oddgeir Friborg, Catharina E. Wang, David Trafimow, and Kristin Woolf, "Mental Habits: Metacognitive Reflection on Negative Self-Thinking," *Journal of Personality and Social Psychology* 92, no. 3 (2007): 526–41, https://doi.org/10.1037/0022-3514.92.3.526.

11. Susan M. Andersen, Gordon B. Moskowitz, Irene V. Blair, and Brian A. Nosek, "Automatic Thought," in *Social Psychology: Handbook of Basic Principles,* 2nd ed., eds. Arie W. Kruglanski and E. Tory Higgins (New York: Guilford Press, 2007), 138–75.

12. Steven Shearer and Lauren Gordon, "The Patient with Excessive Worry," *American Family Physician* 73, no. 6 (March 15, 2006): 20–28, https://doi.org/10.1002/jclp .10028.

13. Steven C. Hayes, Kirk D. Strosahl, and Kelly G. Wilson, *Acceptance and Commitment Therapy: The Process and Practice of Mindful Change* (New York: Guilford Press, 2011).

14. Brian C. Pilecki and Dean McKay, "An Experimental Investigation of Cognitive Defusion," *The Psychological Record* 62 (2012): 19–40, https://doi.org/10.1007 /BF03395784.

15. Francisco J. Ruiz, Bárbara Gil-Luciano, and Miguel A. Segura-Vargas, "Cognitive Defusion," in *The Oxford Handbook of Acceptance and Commitment Therapy,* eds. Michael P. Twohig, Michael E. Levin, and Julie M. Petersen (New York: Oxford University Press, 2023), 206–29.

Chapter 5: Engage the Power of the Present to Get Unstuck

1. Brian T. McMahon, "An Overview of Workplace Discrimination and Disability," *Journal of Vocational Rehabilitation* 36, no. 3 (2012): 135–39, https://doi.org /10.3233/JVR-2012-0588.

2. Ronald L. Simons, Man-Kit Lei, Eric Klopack, Yue Zhang, Frederick X. Gibbons, and Steven R. H. Beach, "Racial Discrimination, Inflammation, and Chronic Illness Among African American Women at Midlife: Support for the Weathering Perspective," *Journal of Racial and Ethnic Health Disparities* 8 (2021): 339–49, https://doi.org/10.1007%2Fs40615-020-00786-8.

3. Gilbert C. Gee, Michael S. Spencer, Juan Chen, and David Takeuchi, "A Nationwide Study of Discrimination and Chronic Health Conditions Among Asian Americans," *American Journal of Public Health* 97, no. 7 (2007): 1275–82, https://doi.org/10.2105%2FAJPH.2006.091827.

4. Thu T. Nguyen, Anusha M. Vable, M. Maria Glymour, and Amani Nuru-Jeter, "Trends for Reported Discrimination in Health Care in a National Sample of Older Adults with Chronic Conditions," *Journal of General Internal Medicine* 33 (2018): 291–97, https://doi.org/10.1007%2Fs11606-017-4209-5.

5. M. McGoldrick, "Therapists, Understanding of the Client-Reported Phenomenon of Feeling Stuck" (PhD diss., City University of London, 2018), https:// openaccess.city.ac.uk/id/eprint/22078.

6. James M. Olson, "Psychological Barriers to Behavior Change: How to Identify the Barriers That Inhibit Change," *Canadian Family Physician* 38 (1992): 309–19, www.ncbi.nlm.nih.gov/pmc/articles/PMC2145450.

7. Shigehiro Oishi, Jaime L. Kurtz, Felicity F. Miao, Jina Park, and Erin Whitchurch, "The Role of Familiarity in Daily Well-Being: Developmental and Cultural Variation," *Developmental Psychology* 47, no. 6 (2011): 1750–56, https://doi.org/10.1037/a0025305.

8. James J. Lucas and Kathleen Anne Moore, "Psychological Flexibility: Positive Implications for Mental Health and Life Satisfaction," *Health Promotion International* 35, no. 2 (2020): 312–20, https://doi.org/10.1093/heapro/daz036.

9. Gera E. Nagelhout, Lette Hogeling, Renate Spruijt, Nathalie Postma, and Hein De Vries, "Barriers and Facilitators for Health Behavior Change Among Adults from Multi-Problem Households: A Qualitative Study," *International Journal of Environmental Research and Public Health* 14, no. 10 (2017): 1229, https://doi.org/10.3390/ijerph14101229.

10. Fred C. Lunenburg, "Goal-Setting Theory of Motivation," *International Journal of Management, Business, and Administration* 15, no. 1 (2011): 1–6, www.nationalforum.com/Electronic%20Journal%20Volumes/Lunenburg,%20Fred%20C.%20Goal-Setting%20Theoryof%20Motivation%20IJMBA%20V15%20N1%202011.pdf.

11. Doug McKenzie-Mohr and P. Wesley Schultz, "Choosing Effective Behavior Change Tools," *Social Marketing Quarterly* 20, no. 1 (2014): 35–46, https://doi.org/10.1177/1524500413519257.

12. Benjamin Tolchin, Gaston Baslet, Steve Martino, Joji Suzuki, Hal Blumenfeld, Lawrence J. Hirsch, Hamada Altalib, et al., "Motivational Interviewing Techniques to Improve Psychotherapy Adherence and Outcomes for Patients with Psychogenic Nonepileptic Seizures," *The Journal of Neuropsychiatry and Clinical Neurosciences* 32, no. 2 (2020): 125–31, https://doi.org/10.1176/appi.neuropsych.19020045.

13. John Teasdale, Mark Williams, and Zindel Segal, *The Mindful Way Workbook: An 8-Week Program to Free Yourself from Depression and Emotional Distress* (New York: Guilford Press, 2013).

14. Ronald D. Siegel, Christopher K. Germer, and Andrew Olendzki, "Mindfulness: What Is It? Where Did It Come From?" in *Clinical Handbook of Mindfulness,* ed. Fabrizio Didonna (New York: Springer, 2010), 17–35, https://doi.org/10.1007/978-0-387-09593-6.

15. Theodoros Karapanagiotidis, Boris C. Bernhardt, Elizabeth Jefferies, and Jonathan Smallwood, "Tracking Thoughts: Exploring the Neural Architecture of Mental Time Travel During Mind-Wandering," *Neuroimage* 147 (2017): 272–81, https://doi.org/10.1016/j.neuroimage.2016.12.031.

16. Edward R. Watkins and Henrietta Roberts, "Reflecting on Rumination: Consequences, Causes, Mechanisms and Treatment of Rumination," *Behaviour Research and Therapy* 127 (2020): 103573, https://doi.org/10.1016/j.brat.2020.103573.

17. J. Mark G. Williams, "Mindfulness, Depression and Modes of Mind," *Cognitive Therapy and Research* 32 (2008): 721–33, https://doi.org/10.1007/s10608-008 -9204-z, https://ocbs.org/wp-content/uploads/2015/09/wms2008modesmind.pdf.
18. Shauna Shapiro, Ronald Siegel, and Kristin D. Neff. "Paradoxes of Mindfulness," *Mindfulness* 9 (2018): 1693–1701, https://doi.org/10.1007/s12671-018-0957-5.
19. Cheng-Kar Phang, Shian-Ling Keng, and Kuei-Chun Chiang, "Mindful-STOP: Mindfulness Made Easy for Stress Reduction in Medical Students," *Education in Medicine Journal* 6, no. 2 (2014), 48–56, https://doi.org/10.5959/eimj .v6i2.230.

Chapter 6: Live Your Values to Enhance Quality of Life

1. Martin J. Fegg, Maria Wasner, Christian Neudert, and Gian Domenico Borasio, "Personal Values and Individual Quality of Life in Palliative Care Patients," *Journal of Pain and Symptom Management* 30, no. 2 (2005): 154–59, https://doi.org /10.1016/j.jpainsymman.2005.02.012.
2. Leila Ahmadi Ghahnaviyeh, Bagherian Bagherian, Awat Feizi, Atefe Afshari, and Firoozeh Mostafavi Darani, "The Effectiveness of Acceptance and Commitment Therapy on Quality of Life in a Patient with Myocardial Infarction: A Randomized Control Trial," *Iranian Journal of Psychiatry* 15, no. 1 (2020): 1–9, https://doi.org/10.18502/ijps.v15i1.2434.
3. Russ Harris, *The Happiness Trap: How to Stop Struggling and Start Living* (Boulder, CO: Shambhala, 2022).
4. Franz J. Vesely, "Alleged Quote," Viktor Frankl Institut, n.d., www.viktorfrankl.org /quote_stimulus.html.

Chapter 7: Harness Empathy for Post-Traumatic Growth

1. Changming Duan and Clara E. Hill, "The Current State of Empathy Research," *Journal of Counseling Psychology* 43, no. 3 (1996): 261–74, https://doi.org/10.1037 /0022-0167.43.3.261.
2. Amanda M. Ferguson, C. Daryl Cameron, and Michael Inzlicht, "When Does Empathy Feel Good?" *Current Opinion in Behavioral Sciences* 39 (2021): 125–29, https://doi.org/10.1016/j.cobeha.2021.03.011.
3. Gal Hayuni, Ilanit Hasson-Ohayon, Gil Goldzweig, Gil Bar Sela, and Michal Braun, "Between Empathy and Grief: The Mediating Effect of Compassion Fatigue Among Oncologists." *Psycho-Oncology* 28, no. 12 (2019): 2344–50, https://doi.org/10.1002/pon.5227.
4. Takuya Yoshiike, Francesco Benedetti, Yoshiya Moriguchi, Benedetta Vai, Veronica Aggio, Keiko Asano, Masaya Ito, et al., "Exploring the Role of Empathy in Prolonged Grief Reactions to Bereavement," *Scientific Reports* 13, no. 1 (2023): 7596, https://doi.org/10.1038/s41598-023-34755-y.

5. Caroline Debnar, Valerie Carrard, Davide Morselli, Gisela Michel, Nicole Bachmann, and Claudio Peter, "Psychological Distress Trajectories in Chronic Physical Health Conditions," *Health Psychology* 39, no. 2 (2020): 116–26, https://doi.org/10.1037/hea0000820, https://eprints.whiterose.ac.uk/157645/1/Debnar_2019_HealthPsychology_Trajectories_accepted.pdf.

6. Richard G. Tedeschi and Lawrence G. Calhoun. *Trauma and Transformation: Growing in the Aftermath of Suffering* (Thousand Oaks, CA: Sage, 1995).

7. Richard G. Tedeschi, Crystal L. Park, and Lawrence G. Calhoun, eds. *Posttraumatic Growth: Positive Changes in the Aftermath of Crisis* (Mahwah, NJ: Lawrence Erlbaum, 1998).

Chapter 8: Connect with Your Body

1. Rune Bang Leistad, T. Sand, R. H. Westgaard, K. B. Nilsen, and L. J. Stovner, "Stress-Induced Pain and Muscle Activity in Patients with Migraine and Tension-Type Headache," *Cephalalgia* 26, no. 1 (2006): 64–73, https://doi.org/10.1111/j.1468-2982.2005.00997.x.

2. A. G. Glaros, J. M. Marszalek, and K. B. Williams, "Longitudinal Multilevel Modeling of Facial Pain, Muscle Tension, and Stress," *Journal of Dental Research* 95, no. 4 (2016): 416–22, https://doi.org/10.1177%2F0022034515625216.

3. Hidetaka Hamasaki, "Effects of Diaphragmatic Breathing on Health: A Narrative Review," *Medicines* 7, no. 10 (2020): 65, https://doi.org/10.3390%2Fmedicines7100065.

4. Shaun Gallagher, "Multiple Aspects in the Sense of Agency," *New Ideas in Psychology* 30, no. 1 (2012): 15–31, https://doi.org/10.1016/j.newideapsych.2010.03.003.

5. Felipe Barreto Schuch and Davy Vancampfort, "Physical Activity, Exercise, and Mental Disorders: It Is Time to Move On," *Trends in Psychiatry and Psychotherapy* 43, no. 3 (2021): 177–84, https://doi.org/10.47626/2237-6089-2021-0237; Kerri A. Morgan, Kelly L. Taylor, Carla Wilson Walker, Susan Tucker, Jessica L. Dashner, and Holly Hollingsworth, "Mobility Disability and Exercise: Health Outcomes of an Accessible Community-Based Center," *Frontiers in Rehabilitation Sciences* 3 (2022): 836655, https://doi.org/10.3389%2Ffresc.2022.836655.

6. Timothy W. Puetz, Patrick J. O'Connor, and Rod K. Dishman, "Effects of Chronic Exercise on Feelings of Energy and Fatigue: A Quantitative Synthesis," *Psychological Bulletin* 132, no. 6 (2006): 866–76, https://doi.org/10.1037/0033-2909.132.6.866.

7. Willem J. Kop, Angela Lyden, Ali A. Berlin, Kirsten Ambrose, Cara Olsen, Richard H. Gracely, David A. Williams, et al., "Ambulatory Monitoring of Physical Activity and Symptoms in Fibromyalgia and Chronic Fatigue Syndrome," *Arthritis & Rheumatism* 52, no. 1 (2005): 296–303, https://doi.org/10.1002/art.20779.

8. Kirsten R. Ambrose and Yvonne M. Golightly, "Physical Exercise as Non-Pharmacological Treatment of Chronic Pain: Why and When," *Best Practice & Research: Clinical Rheumatology* 29, no. 1 (2015): 120–30, https://doi.org /10.1016/j.berh.2015.04.022.

9. Timothy W. Puetz, Sara S. Flowers, and Patrick J. O'Connor, "A Randomized Controlled Trial of the Effect of Aerobic Exercise Training on Feelings of Energy and Fatigue in Sedentary Young Adults with Persistent Fatigue," *Psychotherapy and Psychosomatics* 77, no. 3 (2008): 167–74, https://doi.org/10.1159 /000116610.

10. Victor Ng, Wanda Millard, Constance Lebrun, and John Howard, "Low-Intensity Exercise Improves Quality of Life in Patients with Crohn's Disease." *Clinical Journal of Sport Medicine* 17, no. 5 (2007): 384–88, https://doi.org/10.1097/jsm .0b013e31802b4fda.

Chapter 9: Tolerate Discomfort and Acknowledge the Complexity of Your Experience

1. F. Curtis Breslin, C. Gail Hepburn, Selahadin Ibrahim, and Donald Cole, "Understanding Stability and Change in Psychological Distress and Sense of Coherence: A Four-Year Prospective Study," *Journal of Applied Social Psychology* 36, no. 1 (2006): 1–21, https://psycnet.apa.org/doi/10.1111/j.0021-9029.2006.00001.x.

2. Sharon Dekel, Tsachi Ein-Dor, and Zahava Solomon, "Posttraumatic Growth and Posttraumatic Distress: A Longitudinal Study," *Psychological Trauma: Theory, Research, Practice, and Policy* 4, no. 1 (2012): 94–101, https://doi.org/10.1037 /a0021865.

3. Henriët van Middendorp, Mark A. Lumley, Johannes W. G. Jacobs, Lorenz J. P. van Doornen, Johannes W. J. Bijlsma, and Rinie Geenen, "Emotions and Emotional Approach and Avoidance Strategies in Fibromyalgia," *Journal of Psychosomatic Research* 64, no. 2 (2008): 159–67, https://doi.org/10.1016/j.jpsychores.2007.08.009.

4. JoAnne Dahl and Tobias Lundgren, *Living Beyond Your Pain: Using Acceptance and Commitment Therapy to Ease Chronic Pain* (Oakland, CA: New Harbinger, 2006).

5. Todd B. Kashdan and Jonathan Rottenberg, "Psychological Flexibility as a Fundamental Aspect of Health," *Clinical Psychology Review* 30, no. 7 (2010): 865–78, https://doi.org/10.1016%2Fj.cpr.2010.03.001.

Chapter 10: Give Yourself Permission to Do Things Differently

1. Nurit Weinblatt and Michal Avrech-Bar, "Rest: A Qualitative Exploration of the Phenomenon," *Occupational Therapy International* 10, no. 4 (2003): 227–38, https://doi.org/10.1002/oti.187.

2. Alan Baron and Mark Galizio, "Positive and Negative Reinforcement: Should the Distinction Be Preserved?" *The Behavior Analyst* 28 (2005): 85–98, https://doi.org/10.1007%2FBF03392107.

3. Renata Hadzic, Louise Sharpe, and Bradley M. Wood, "The Relationship Between Pacing and Avoidance in Chronic Pain: A Systematic Review and Meta-Analysis," *The Journal of Pain* 18, no. 10 (2017): 1165–73, https://doi.org/10.1016/j.jpain.2017.04.008.

4. Abby Hershler, "Window of Tolerance," in *Looking at Trauma: A Tool Kit for Clinicians,* eds. Abby Hershler, Lesley Hughes, Patricia Nguyen, and Shelley Wall (University Park, PA: Pennsylvania State University Press, 2021), 25–28, https://doi.org/10.5325/j.ctv1wmz3qr.

5. Mirco Rogg, Diana Braakmann, Anja Schaich, Julia Ambrosch, Clara Meine, Nele Assmann, Ulrich Schweiger, et al., "How Patients with Borderline Personality Disorder Experience the Skill Opposite Action in the Context of Dialectical Behavior Therapy—A Qualitative Study," *Psychotherapy* 58, no. 4 (2021): 544–56, https://doi.org/10.1037/pst0000392.

6. Marsha M. Linehan, *DBT Skills Training Manual,* 2nd ed. (New York: Guilford Press, 2014).

Bibliography

Ahlström, Gerd. "Experiences of Loss and Chronic Sorrow in Persons with Severe Chronic Illness." *Journal of Clinical Nursing* 16, no. 3a (2007): 76–83. https://doi.org/10.1111/j.1365-2702.2006.01580.x.

Aldao, Amelia, and Andre J. Plate. "Coping and Emotion Regulation." In *Process-Based CBT: The Science and Core Clinical Competencies of Cognitive Behavioral Therapy*, edited by S. C. Hayes and S. G. Hofmann. Oakland, CA: New Harbinger, 2018.

Ambrose, Kirsten R., and Yvonne M. Golightly. "Physical Exercise as Non-Pharmacological Treatment of Chronic Pain: Why and When." *Best Practice & Research: Clinical Rheumatology* 29, no. 1 (2015): 120–30. https://doi.org/10.1016/j.berh.2015.04.022.

Andersen, Susan M., Gordon B. Moskowitz, Irene V. Blair, and Brian A. Nosek. "Automatic Thought." In *Social Psychology: Handbook of Basic Principles*, 2nd ed., edited by Arie W. Kruglanski and E. Tory Higgins. New York: Guilford Press, 2007.

Baron, Alan, and Mark Galizio. "Positive and Negative Reinforcement: Should the Distinction Be Preserved?" *The Behavior Analyst* 28 (2005): 85–98. https://doi.org/10.1007%2FBF03392107.

Breslin, F. Curtis, C. Gail Hepburn, Selahadin Ibrahim, and Donald Cole. "Understanding Stability and Change in Psychological Distress and Sense of Coherence: A Four-Year Prospective Study." *Journal of Applied Social Psychology* 36, no. 1 (2006): 1–21. https://psycnet.apa.org/doi/10.1111/j.0021-9029.2006.00001.x.

Bueno-Gómez, Noelia. "Conceptualizing Suffering and Pain." *Philosophy, Ethics, and Humanities in Medicine* 12 (2017): 1–11. https://doi.org/10.1186/s13010-017-0049-5.

Buschmann, Tim, Robert A. Horn, Virginia R. Blankenship, Y. Evie Garcia, and Kathy B. Bohan. "The Relationship Between Automatic Thoughts and Irrational Beliefs Predicting Anxiety and Depression." *Journal of Rational-Emotive & Cognitive-Behavior Therapy* 36 (2018): 137–62. https://doi.org/10.1007/s10942-017-0278-y.

Carver, Charles S., and Michael F. Scheier. "Dispositional Optimism." *Trends in Cognitive Sciences* 18, no. 6 (2014): 293–99. https://doi.org/10.1016%2Fj.tics.2014.02.003.

Cast, Alicia D., and Peter J. Burke. "A Theory of Self-Esteem." *Social Forces* 80, no. 3 (2002): 1041–68. https://doi.org/10.1353/sof.2002.0003.

Clore, Gerald L., and Jeffrey R. Huntsinger. "How Emotions Inform Judgment and Regulate Thought." *Trends in Cognitive Sciences* 11, no. 9 (2007): 393–99. https://doi.org/10.1016/j.tics.2007.08.005.

Cordova, James V. "Acceptance in Behavior Therapy: Understanding the Process of Change." *The Behavior Analyst* 24 (2001): 213–26. https://doi.org/10.1007 %2FBF03392032.

Dahl, JoAnne, and Tobias Lundgren. *Living Beyond Your Pain: Using Acceptance and Commitment Therapy to Ease Chronic Pain.* Oakland, CA: New Harbinger, 2006.

de Vries, Reinout E., Jeroen Pronk, Tjeert Olthof, and Frits A. Goossens. "Getting Along and/or Getting Ahead: Differential HEXACO Personality Correlates of Likeability and Popularity Among Adolescents." *European Journal of Personality* 34, no. 2 (2020): 245–61. https://doi.org/10.1002/per.2243.

Debnar, Caroline, Valerie Carrard, Davide Morselli, Gisela Michel, Nicole Bachmann, and Claudio Peter. "Psychological Distress Trajectories in Chronic Physical Health Conditions." *Health Psychology* 39, no. 2 (2020): 116–26. https://doi.org/10.1037/hea0000820. https://eprints.whiterose.ac.uk/157645/1 /Debnar_2019_HealthPsychology_Trajectories_accepted.pdf.

Dekel, Sharon, Tsachi Ein-Dor, and Zahava Solomon. "Posttraumatic Growth and Posttraumatic Distress: A Longitudinal Study." *Psychological Trauma: Theory, Research, Practice, and Policy* 4, no. 1 (2012): 94–101. https://doi.org/10.1037 /a0021865.

Desmond, Tim. *Self-Compassion in Psychotherapy: Mindfulness Based Practices for Healing and Transformation.* New York: W. W. Norton, 2016.

Dixon-Gordon, Katherine L., Amelia Aldao, and Andres De Los Reyes. "Emotion Regulation in Context: Examining the Spontaneous Use of Strategies Across Emotional Intensity and Type of Emotion." *Personality and Individual Differences* 86 (2015): 271–76. https://doi.org/10.1016/j.paid.2015.06.011.

Dryden, Windy. "Unconditional Self-Acceptance and Self-Compassion." In *The Strength of Self-Acceptance: Theory, Practice and Research,* edited by Michael E. Bernard. New York: Springer, 2013. https://doi.org/10.1007/978-1-4614-6806-6_7.

Duan, Changming, and Clara E. Hill. "The Current State of Empathy Research." *Journal of Counseling Psychology* 43, no. 3 (1996): 261–74. https://doi.org /10.1037/0022-0167.43.3.261.

Ellis, Albert. "Psychotherapy and the Value of a Human Being." In *Handbook of Rational-Emotive Therapy,* edited by Albert Ellis and Russell Grieger. New York: Springer, 1977.

Emmons, Robert A. *Thanks!: How the New Science of Gratitude Can Make You Happier.* Boston: Houghton Mifflin Harcourt, 2007.

Fegg, Martin J., Maria Wasner, Christian Neudert, and Gian Domenico Borasio. "Personal Values and Individual Quality of Life in Palliative Care Patients." *Journal of Pain and Symptom Management* 30, no. 2 (2005): 154–59. https://doi.org/10.1016/j.jpainsymman.2005.02.012.

Feldman, Benjamin G. "How Do Mindfulness Practitioners Describe Pausing?: A Qualitative Interview Study." *Bridgewater State University Undergraduate Review* 14 (2018): 41–54. https://vc.bridgew.edu/cgi/viewcontent.cgi?article=1437&context=undergrad_rev.

Ferguson, Amanda M., C. Daryl Cameron, and Michael Inzlicht. "When Does Empathy Feel Good?" *Current Opinion in Behavioral Sciences* 39 (2021): 125–29. https://doi.org/10.1016/j.cobeha.2021.03.011.

Freeston, Mark, Ashley Tiplady, Lauren Mawn, Gioia Bottesi, and Sarah Thwaites. "Towards a Model of Uncertainty Distress in the Context of Coronavirus (COVID-19)." *The Cognitive Behaviour Therapist* 13 (2020): e31. https://doi.org/10.1017%2FS1754470X2000029X.

Gallagher, Shaun. "Multiple Aspects in the Sense of Agency." *New Ideas in Psychology* 30, no. 1 (2012): 15–31. https://doi.org/10.1016/j.newideapsych.2010.03.003.

Gasper, Karen, and Cinnamon L. Danube. "The Scope of Our Affective Influences: When and How Naturally Occurring Positive, Negative, and Neutral Affects Alter Judgment." *Personality and Social Psychology Bulletin* 42, no. 3 (2016): 385–99. https://doi.org/10.1177/0146167216629131.

Gee, Gilbert C., Michael S. Spencer, Juan Chen, and David Takeuchi. "A Nationwide Study of Discrimination and Chronic Health Conditions Among Asian Americans." *American Journal of Public Health* 97, no. 7 (2007): 1275–82. https://doi.org/10.2105%2FAJPH.2006.091827.

Germer, Christopher K., and Kristin D. Neff. "Self-Compassion in Clinical Practice." *Journal of Clinical Psychology* 69, no. 8 (2013): 856–67. https://doi.org/10.1002/jclp.22021.

Ghahnaviyeh, Leila Ahmadi, Bagherian Bagherian, Awat Feizi, Atefe Afshari, and Firoozeh Mostafavi Darani. "The Effectiveness of Acceptance and Commitment Therapy on Quality of Life in a Patient with Myocardial Infarction: A Randomized Control Trial." *Iranian Journal of Psychiatry* 15, no. 1 (2020): 1–9. https://doi.org/10.18502/ijps.v15i1.2434.

Glaros, A. G., J. M. Marszalek, and K. B. Williams. "Longitudinal Multilevel Modeling of Facial Pain, Muscle Tension, and Stress." *Journal of Dental Research* 95, no. 4 (2016): 416–22. https://doi.org/10.1177%2F0022034515625216.

Gross, James J., and Oliver P. John. "Individual Differences in Two Emotion Regulation Processes: Implications for Affect, Relationships, and Well-Being." *Journal of Personality and Social Psychology* 85, no. 2 (2003): 348–62. https://doi.org/10.1037/0022-3514.85.2.348.

Hadzic, Renata, Louise Sharpe, and Bradley M. Wood. "The Relationship Between Pacing and Avoidance in Chronic Pain: A Systematic Review and Meta-Analysis." *The Journal of Pain* 18, no. 10 (2017): 1165–73. https://doi.org/10.1016/j.jpain.2017.04.008.

Hamasaki, Hidetaka. "Effects of Diaphragmatic Breathing on Health: A Narrative Review." *Medicines* 7, no. 10 (2020): 65. https://doi.org/10.3390%2Fmedicines7100065.

Harris, Russ. *ACT Made Simple: An Easy-to-Read Primer on Acceptance and Commitment Therapy.* Oakland, CA: New Harbinger, 2019.

Harris, Russ. *The Happiness Trap: How to Stop Struggling and Start Living.* Boulder, CO: Shambhala, 2022.

Hayes, Steven C., Jason B. Luoma, Frank W. Bond, Akihiko Masuda, and Jason Lillis. "Acceptance and Commitment Therapy: Model, Processes and Outcomes." *Behaviour Research and Therapy* 44, no. 1 (2006): 1–25. https://doi.org/10.1016/j.brat.2005.06.006.

Hayes, Steven C., Kirk D. Strosahl, and Kelly G. Wilson. *Acceptance and Commitment Therapy: The Process and Practice of Mindful Change.* New York: Guilford Press, 2011.

Hayuni, Gal, Ilanit Hasson-Ohayon, Gil Goldzweig, Gil Bar Sela, and Michal Braun. "Between Empathy and Grief: The Mediating Effect of Compassion Fatigue Among Oncologists." *Psycho-Oncology* 28, no. 12 (2019): 2344–50. https://doi.org/10.1002/pon.5227.

Hershler, Abby. "Window of Tolerance." In *Looking at Trauma: A Tool Kit for Clinicians,* edited by Abby Hershler, Lesley Hughes, Patricia Nguyen, and Shelley Wall. University Park, PA: Pennsylvania State University Press, 2021. https://doi.org/10.5325/j.ctv1wmz3qr.

Herzberg, Kristin N., Sean C. Sheppard, John P. Forsyth, Marcus Credé, Mitch Earleywine, and Georg H. Eifert. "The Believability of Anxious Feelings and Thoughts Questionnaire (BAFT): A Psychometric Evaluation of Cognitive Fusion in a Nonclinical and Highly Anxious Community Sample." *Psychological Assessment* 24, no. 4 (2012): 877–91. https://doi.org/10.1037/a0027782.

Hjemdal, Odin, Tore Stiles, and Adrian Wells. "Automatic Thoughts and Meta-Cognition as Predictors of Depressive or Anxious Symptoms: A Prospective Study of Two Trajectories." *Scandinavian Journal of Psychology* 54, no. 2 (2013): 59–65. https://doi.org/10.1111/sjop.12010.

Hoffman Institute Foundation. "Feelings List." 2013. www.hoffmaninstitute.org/wp-content/uploads/Practices-FeelingsSensations.pdf.

Ito, Tiffany A., Jeff T. Larsen, N. Kyle Smith, and John T. Cacioppo. "Negative Information Weighs More Heavily on the Brain: The Negativity Bias in Evaluative Categorizations." *Journal of Personality and Social Psychology* 75, no. 4 (1998): 887. https://doi.org/10.1037//0022-3514.75.4.887.

Karapanagiotidis, Theodoros, Boris C. Bernhardt, Elizabeth Jefferies, and Jonathan Smallwood. "Tracking Thoughts: Exploring the Neural Architecture of Mental Time Travel During Mind-Wandering." *Neuroimage* 147 (2017): 272–81. https://doi.org/10.1016/j.neuroimage.2016.12.031.

Kashdan, Todd B., and Jonathan Rottenberg. "Psychological Flexibility as a Fundamental Aspect of Health." *Clinical Psychology Review* 30, no. 7 (2010): 865–78. https://doi.org/10.1016%2Fj.cpr.2010.03.001.

Kohn, Nils, T. Toygar, C. Weidenfeld, M. Berthold-Losleben, N. Chechko, S. Orfanos, S. Vocke, A. Durst, Z. G. Laoutidis, W. Karges, F. Schneider, and U. Habel. "In a Sweet Mood? Effects of Experimental Modulation of Blood Glucose Levels on Mood-Induction During fMRI." *Neuroimage* 113 (2015): 246–56. https://doi .org/10.1016/j.neuroimage.2015.03.024.

Kop, Willem J., Angela Lyden, Ali A. Berlin, Kirsten Ambrose, Cara Olsen, Richard H. Gracely, David A. Williams, and Daniel J. Clauw. "Ambulatory Monitoring of Physical Activity and Symptoms in Fibromyalgia and Chronic Fatigue Syndrome." *Arthritis & Rheumatism* 52, no. 1 (2005): 296–303. https://doi.org/10.1002/art.20779.

Kozubal, Magdalena, Anna Szuster, and Adrianna Wielgopolan. "Emotional Regulation Strategies in Daily Life: The Intensity of Emotions and Regulation Choice." *Frontiers in Psychology* 14 (August 13, 2023): 1218694. https://doi.org/10.3389 /fpsyg.2023.1218694.

Landoni, Marta, Milica Petrovic, Chiara Ionio, and Andrea Gaggioli. "Vulnerability and Informal Caregiver: A Scoping Review." *medRxiv* (2021). https://doi.org /10.1101/2021.09.02.21263030.

Leary, Mark R., Eleanor B. Tate, Claire E. Adams, Ashley Batts Allen, and Jessica Hancock. "Self-Compassion and Reactions to Unpleasant Self-Relevant Events: The Implications of Treating Oneself Kindly." *Journal of Personality and Social Psychology* 92, no. 5 (2007): 887. https://doi.org/10.1037/0022-3514.92.5.887.

Lebel, Sophie, Brittany Mutsaers, Christina Tomei, Caroline Séguin Leclair, Georden Jones, Danielle Petricone-Westwood, Nicole Rutkowski, Viviane Ta, Geneviève Trudel, Simone Zofia Laflamme, et al. "Health Anxiety and Illness-Related Fears Across Diverse Chronic Illnesses: A Systematic Review on Conceptualization, Measurement, Prevalence, Course, and Correlates." *PloS One* 15, no. 7 (2020): e0234124. https://doi.org/10.1371/journal.pone.0234124.

Lee, Joy Yeonjoo, Adam Szulewski, John Q. Young, Jeroen Donkers, Halszka Jarodzka, and Jeroen J. G. van Merriënboer. "The Medical Pause: Importance, Processes and Training." *Medical Education* 55, no. 10 (2021): 1152–60. https://doi.org /10.1111/medu.14529.

Leistad, Rune Bang, T. Sand, R. H. Westgaard, K. B. Nilsen, and L. J. Stovner. "Stress-Induced Pain and Muscle Activity in Patients with Migraine and Tension-Type Headache." *Cephalalgia* 26, no. 1 (2006): 64–73. https://doi.org /10.1111/j.1468-2982.2005.00997.x.

Lestari, Rini, and Maharani Fajar. "Gratitude, Self-Esteem and Optimism in People with Physical Disabilities." *Prizren Social Science Journal* 4, no. 2 (2020): 14–21. https://doi.org/10.32936/pssj.v4i2.150.

Linehan, Marsha M. *Building a Life Worth Living: A Memoir.* New York: Random House, 2021.

Linehan, Marsha M. *DBT Skills Training Manual,* 2nd ed. New York: Guilford Press, 2014.

Lucas, James J., and Kathleen Anne Moore. "Psychological Flexibility: Positive Implications for Mental Health and Life Satisfaction." *Health Promotion International* 35, no. 2 (2020): 312–20. https://doi.org/10.1093/heapro/daz036.

Lunenburg, Fred C. "Goal-Setting Theory of Motivation." *International Journal of Management, Business, and Administration* 15, no. 1 (2011): 1–6. www.national forum.com/Electronic%20Journal%20Volumes/Lunenburg,%20Fred%20C.%20 Goal-Setting%20Theoryof%20Motivation%20IJMBA%20V15%20N1%202011.pdf.

Lupton, Deborah, and John Tulloch. "'Life Would Be Pretty Dull Without Risk': Voluntary Risk-Taking and Its Pleasures." *Health, Risk & Society* 4, no. 2 (2002): 113–24. https://doi.org/10.1080/13698570220137015.

Mackenzie, Catriona, Wendy Rogers, and Susan Dodds. "Introduction: What Is Vulnerability and Why Does It Matter for Moral Theory." In *Vulnerability: New Essays in Ethics and Feminist Philosophy.* New York: Oxford University Press, 2014.

Masento, Natalie A., Mark Golightly, David T. Field, Laurie T. Butler, and Carien M. van Reekum. "Effects of Hydration Status on Cognitive Performance and Mood." *British Journal of Nutrition* 111, no. 10 (2014): 1841–52. https://doi.org/10.1017/S0007114513004455.

Maslow, A. H. "A Theory of Human Motivation." *Psychological Review* 50:4 (1943): 370–96. https://doi.org/10.1037/h0054346, https://psychclassics.yorku.ca/Maslow/motivation.htm.

McBride, Hillary L. *The Wisdom of Your Body: Finding Healing, Wholeness, and Connection Through Embodied Living.* Ada, MI: Brazos Press, 2021.

McGoldrick, M. "Therapists, Understanding of the Client-Reported Phenomenon of Feeling Stuck." PhD diss., City University of London, 2018. https://openaccess.city.ac.uk/id/eprint/22078.

McKenzie-Mohr, Doug, and P. Wesley Schultz. "Choosing Effective Behavior Change Tools." *Social Marketing Quarterly* 20, no. 1 (2014): 35–46. https://doi.org/10.1177/1524500413519257.

McMahon, Brian T. "An Overview of Workplace Discrimination and Disability." *Journal of Vocational Rehabilitation* 36, no. 3 (2012): 135–39. https://doi.org/10.3233/JVR-2012-0588.

Mekawi, Yara, Sierra Carter, Grace Packard, Shimarith Wallace, Vasiliki Michopoulos, and Abigail Powers. "When (Passive) Acceptance Hurts: Race-Based Coping Moderates the Association Between Racial Discrimination and

Mental Health Outcomes Among Black Americans." *Psychological Trauma: Theory, Research, Practice, and Policy* 14, no. 1 (2022): 38. https://doi.org/10.1037/tra0001077.

Morgan, Kerri A., Kelly L. Taylor, Carla Wilson Walker, Susan Tucker, Jessica L. Dashner, and Holly Hollingsworth. "Mobility Disability and Exercise: Health Outcomes of an Accessible Community-Based Center." *Frontiers in Rehabilitation Sciences* 3 (2022): 836655. https://doi.org/10.3389%2Ffresc.2022.836655.

Morone, Natalia E., Cheryl P. Lynch, Vincent J. Losasso, Karl Liebe, and Carol M. Greco. "Mindfulness to Reduce Psychosocial Stress." *Mindfulness* 3 (2012): 22–29. https://doi.org/10.1007/s12671-011-0076-z.

Nagelhout, Gera E., Lette Hogeling, Renate Spruijt, Nathalie Postma, and Hein De Vries. "Barriers and Facilitators for Health Behavior Change Among Adults from Multi-Problem Households: A Qualitative Study." *International Journal of Environmental Research and Public Health* 14, no. 10 (2017): 1229. https://doi.org/10.3390/ijerph14101229.

Neff, Kristin D. "The Development and Validation of a Scale to Measure Self-Compassion." *Self and Identity* 2, no. 3 (2003): 223–50. https://doi.org/10.1080/15298860390209035.

Nes, Lise Solberg, Shawna L. Ehlers, Mary O. Whipple, and Ann Vincent. "Self-Regulatory Fatigue in Chronic Multisymptom Illnesses: Scale Development, Fatigue, and Self-Control." *Journal of Pain Research* 2013 (6): 181–88. https://doi.org/10.2147/JPR.S40014.

Ng, Victor, Wanda Millard, Constance Lebrun, and John Howard. "Low-Intensity Exercise Improves Quality of Life in Patients with Crohn's Disease." *Clinical Journal of Sport Medicine* 17, no. 5 (2007): 384–88. https://doi.org/10.1097/jsm.0b013e31802b4fda.

Nguyen, Thu T., Anusha M. Vable, M. Maria Glymour, and Amani Nuru-Jeter. "Trends for Reported Discrimination in Health Care in a National Sample of Older Adults with Chronic Conditions." *Journal of General Internal Medicine* 33 (2018): 291–97. https://doi.org/10.1007%2Fs11606-017-4209-5.

Oishi, Shigehiro, Jaime L. Kurtz, Felicity F. Miao, Jina Park, and Erin Whitchurch. "The Role of Familiarity in Daily Well-Being: Developmental and Cultural Variation." *Developmental Psychology* 47, no. 6 (2011): 1750–56. https://doi.org/10.1037/a0025305.

Olson, James M. "Psychological Barriers to Behavior Change: How to Identify the Barriers That Inhibit Change." *Canadian Family Physician* 38 (1992): 309–19. www.ncbi.nlm.nih.gov/pmc/articles/PMC2145450.

Pakula, Amy Thornhill, Kim Van Naarden Braun, and Marshalyn Yeargin-Allsopp. "Cerebral Palsy: Classification and Epidemiology." *Physical Medicine and Rehabilitation Clinics* 20, no. 3 (2009): 425–52. https://doi.org/10.1016/j.pmr.2009.06.001.

Pellizzer, Mia L., and Tracey D. Wade. "Developing a Definition of Body Neutrality and Strategies for an Intervention." *Body Image* 46 (2023): 434–42. https://doi .org/10.1016/j.bodyim.2023.07.006.

Phang, Cheng-Kar, Shian-Ling Keng, and Kuei-Chun Chiang. "Mindful-STOP: Mindfulness Made Easy for Stress Reduction in Medical Students." *Education in Medicine Journal* 6, no. 2 (2014): 48–56. https://doi.org/10.5959/eimj.v6i2.230.

Pietromonaco, Paula R., Bert Uchino, and Christine Dunkel Schetter. "Close Relationship Processes and Health: Implications of Attachment Theory for Health and Disease." *Health Psychology* 32, no. 5 (2013): 499. https://doi.org/10.1037 %2Fa0029349.

Pilecki, Brian C., and Dean McKay. "An Experimental Investigation of Cognitive Defusion." *The Psychological Record* 62 (2012): 19–40. https://doi.org/10.1007 /BF03395784.

Pinheiro, Patrícia, Miguel M. Gonçalves, Daniela Nogueira, Rui Pereira, Isabel Basto, Daniela Alves, and João Salgado. "Emotional Processing During the Therapy for Complicated Grief." *Psychotherapy Research* 32, no. 5 (2022): 678–93. https://doi.org/10.1080/10503307.2021.1985183.

Pleas, Kayleigh, and Cory Muscara. "The Practice of Mindfulness." In *Becoming Mindful: Integrating Mindfulness into Your Psychiatric Practice,* edited by Erin Zerbo, Alan Schlechter, Seema Desai, and Petros Levounis. Washington, DC: American Psychiatric Association, 2016.

Popov, Stanislava, Jelena Radanović, and Mikloš Biro. "Unconditional Self-Acceptance and Mental Health in Ego-Provoking Experimental Context." *Suvremena Psihologija* 19, no. 1 (2016): 71–79. https://doi.org/10.21465/2016-SP-191-06.

Price, Cynthia J., and Carole Hooven. "Interoceptive Awareness Skills for Emotion Regulation: Theory and Approach of Mindful Awareness in Body-Oriented Therapy (MABT)." *Frontiers in Psychology* 9 (May 27, 2018): 335233. https://doi .org/10.3389/fpsyg.2018.00798.

Puetz, Timothy W., Sara S. Flowers, and Patrick J. O'Connor. "A Randomized Controlled Trial of the Effect of Aerobic Exercise Training on Feelings of Energy and Fatigue in Sedentary Young Adults with Persistent Fatigue." *Psychotherapy and Psychosomatics* 77, no. 3 (2008): 167–74. https://doi.org/10.1159/000116610.

Puetz, Timothy W., Patrick J. O'Connor, and Rod K. Dishman. "Effects of Chronic Exercise on Feelings of Energy and Fatigue: A Quantitative Synthesis." *Psychological Bulletin* 132, no. 6 (2006): 866–76. https://doi.org/10.1037/0033-2909 .132.6.866.

Rogg, Mirco, Diana Braakmann, Anja Schaich, Julia Ambrosch, Clara Meine, Nele Assmann, Ulrich Schweiger, and Eva Fassbinder. "How Patients with Borderline Personality Disorder Experience the Skill Opposite Action in the Context of Dialectical Behavior Therapy—A Qualitative Study." *Psychotherapy* 58, no. 4 (2021): 544–56. https://doi.org/10.1037/pst0000392.

Rosenberg, Marshall B., and Deepak Chopra. *Nonviolent Communication: A Language of Life*. Encinitas, CA: PuddleDancer Press, 2015.

Roth, Deborah A., Winnie Eng, and Richard G. Heimberg. "Cognitive Behavior Therapy." In *Encyclopedia of Psychotherapy*, edited by Michel Hersen and William H. Sledge. Washington, DC: American Psychiatric Press, 2002.

Ruiz, Francisco J., Bárbara Gil-Luciano, and Miguel A. Segura-Vargas. "Cognitive Defusion." In *The Oxford Handbook of Acceptance and Commitment Therapy*, edited by Michael P. Twohig, Michael E. Levin, and Julie M. Petersen. New York: Oxford University Press, 2023.

Schroeder, Doris, and Eugenijus Gefenas. "Vulnerability: Too Vague and Too Broad?" *Cambridge Quarterly of Healthcare Ethics* 18, no. 2 (2009): 113–21. https://doi.org/10.1017/S0963180109090203.

Schuch, Felipe Barreto, and Davy Vancampfort. "Physical Activity, Exercise, and Mental Disorders: It Is Time to Move On." *Trends in Psychiatry and Psychotherapy* 43, no. 3 (2021): 177–84. https://doi.org/10.47626/2237-6089-2021-0237.

Schwartz, Jeffrey, and Rebecca Gladding. *You Are Not Your Brain: The 4-Step Solution for Changing Bad Habits, Ending Unhealthy Thinking, and Taking Control of Your Life*. New York: Penguin, 2012.

Scott, Ian A., Jenny A. Doust, Gerben B. Keijzers, and Katharine A. Wallis. "Coping with Uncertainty in Clinical Practice: A Narrative Review." *Medical Journal of Australia* 218, no. 9 (2023). https://doi.org/10.5694/mja2.51925.

Seekis, Veya, and Rebecca K. Lawrence. "How Exposure to Body Neutrality Content on TikTok Affects Young Women's Body Image and Mood." *Body Image* 47 (2023): 101629. https://doi.org/10.1016/j.bodyim.2023.101629.

Shapero, Benjamin G., Lyn Y. Abramson, and Lauren B. Alloy. "Emotional Reactivity and Internalizing Symptoms: Moderating Role of Emotion Regulation." *Cognitive Therapy and Research* 40 (2016): 328–40. https://doi.org/10.1007/s10608-015-9722-4.

Shapiro, Shauna, Ronald Siegel, and Kristin D. Neff. "Paradoxes of Mindfulness." *Mindfulness* 9 (2018): 1693–1701. https://doi.org/10.1007/s12671-018-0957-5.

Shearer, Steven, and Lauren Gordon. "The Patient with Excessive Worry." *American Family Physician* 73, no. 6 (March 15, 2006): 20–28. https://doi.org/10.1002/jclp.10028.

Siegel, Ronald D., Christopher K. Germer, and Andrew Olendzki. "Mindfulness: What Is It? Where Did It Come From?" In *Clinical Handbook of Mindfulness*, edited by Fabrizio Didonna. New York: Springer, 2010. https://doi.org/10.1007/978-0-387-09593-6.

Siler, Shaunna, Tami Borneman, and Betty Ferrell. "Pain and Suffering." *Seminars in Oncology Nursing* 35, no. 3 (June 2019): 310–14. https://doi.org/10.1016/j.soncn.2019.04.013.

Simons, Ronald L., Man-Kit Lei, Eric Klopack, Yue Zhang, Frederick X. Gibbons, and Steven R. H. Beach. "Racial Discrimination, Inflammation, and Chronic Illness Among African American Women at Midlife: Support for the Weathering Perspective." *Journal of Racial and Ethnic Health Disparities* 8 (2021): 339–49. https://doi.org/10.1007%2Fs40615-020-00786-8.

Taleporos, George, and Marita P. McCabe. "Body Image and Physical Disability—Personal Perspectives." *Social Science & Medicine* 54, no. 6 (2002): 971–80. https://doi.org/10.1016/S0277-9536(01)00069-7.

Taylor, Shelley E., Baldwin M. Way, and Teresa E. Seeman. "Early Adversity and Adult Health Outcomes." *Development and Psychopathology* 23, no. 3 (2011): 939–54. https://doi.org/10.1017/S0954579411000411.

Teal, Jeffrey C., and Gary T. Athelstan. "Sexuality and Spinal Cord Injury: Some Psychosocial Considerations." *Archives of Physical Medicine and Rehabilitation* 56, no. 6 (1975): 264–68.

Teasdale, John, Mark Williams, and Zindel Segal. *The Mindful Way Workbook: An 8-Week Program to Free Yourself from Depression and Emotional Distress.* New York: Guilford Press, 2013.

Tedeschi, Richard G., and Lawrence G. Calhoun. *Trauma and Transformation: Growing in the Aftermath of Suffering.* Thousand Oaks, CA: Sage, 1995.

Tedeschi, Richard G., Crystal L. Park, and Lawrence G. Calhoun, eds. *Posttraumatic Growth: Positive Changes in the Aftermath of Crisis.* Mahwah, NJ: Lawrence Erlbaum, 1998.

Ten Klooster, Peter M., Lieke C. A. Christenhusz, Erik Taal, Frank Eggelmeijer, Jan-Maarten van Woerkom, and Johannes J. Rasker. "Feelings of Guilt and Shame in Patients with Rheumatoid Arthritis." *Clinical Rheumatology* 33 (2014): 903–10. https://doi.org/10.1007/s10067-014-2516-3.

Tolchin, Benjamin, Gaston Baslet, Steve Martino, Joji Suzuki, Hal Blumenfeld, Lawrence J. Hirsch, Hamada Altalib, and Barbara A. Dworetzky. "Motivational Interviewing Techniques to Improve Psychotherapy Adherence and Outcomes for Patients with Psychogenic Nonepileptic Seizures." *The Journal of Neuropsychiatry and Clinical Neurosciences* 32, no. 2 (2020): 125–31. https://doi.org/10.1176/appi.neuropsych.19020045.

Van Middendorp, Henriët, Mark A. Lumley, Johannes W. G. Jacobs, Lorenz J. P. van Doornen, Johannes W. J. Bijlsma, and Rinie Geenen. "Emotions and Emotional Approach and Avoidance Strategies in Fibromyalgia." *Journal of Psychosomatic Research* 64, no. 2 (2008): 159–67. https://doi.org/10.1016/j.jpsychores.2007.08.009.

Verplanken, Bas, Oddgeir Friborg, Catharina E. Wang, David Trafimow, and Kristin Woolf. "Mental Habits: Metacognitive Reflection on Negative Self-Thinking." *Journal of Personality and Social Psychology* 92, no. 3 (2007): 526–41. https://doi.org/10.1037/0022-3514.92.3.526.

Vesely, Franz J. "Alleged Quote." Viktor Frankl Institut. N.d. www.viktorfrankl.org /quote_stimulus.html.

Watkins, Edward R., and Henrietta Roberts. "Reflecting on Rumination: Consequences, Causes, Mechanisms and Treatment of Rumination." *Behaviour Research and Therapy* 127 (2020): 103573. https://doi.org/10.1016/j.brat.2020.103573.

Weinblatt, Nurit, and Michal Avrech-Bar. "Rest: A Qualitative Exploration of the Phenomenon." *Occupational Therapy International* 10, no. 4 (2003): 227–38. https://doi.org/10.1002/oti.187.

Werner, Anne, Lise Widding Isaksen, and Kirsti Malterud. "'I Am Not the Kind of Woman Who Complains of Everything': Illness Stories on Self and Shame in Women with Chronic Pain." *Social Science & Medicine* 59, no. 5 (2004): 1035–45. https://doi.org/10.1016/j.socscimed.2003.12.001.

Williams, John C., and Steven Jay Lynn. "Acceptance: An Historical and Conceptual Review." *Imagination, Cognition and Personality* 30, no. 1 (2010): 5–56. https:// doi.org/10.2190/IC.30.1.c.

Williams, J. Mark G. "Mindfulness, Depression and Modes of Mind." *Cognitive Therapy and Research* 32 (2008): 721–33. https://doi.org/10.1007/s10608-008 -9204-z. https://ocbs.org/wp-content/uploads/2015/09/wms2008modesmind.pdf.

Wood, Alex M., Jeffrey J. Froh, and Adam W. A. Geraghty. "Gratitude and Well-Being: A Review and Theoretical Integration." *Clinical Psychology Review* 30, no. 7 (2010): 890–905. https://doi.org/10.1016/j.cpr.2010.03.005.

Yoshiike, Takuya, Francesco Benedetti, Yoshiya Moriguchi, Benedetta Vai, Veronica Aggio, Keiko Asano, Masaya Ito, Hiroki Ikeda, Hidefumi Ohmura, Motoyasu Honma, et al. "Exploring the Role of Empathy in Prolonged Grief Reactions to Bereavement." *Scientific Reports* 13, no. 1 (2023): 7596. https://doi.org/10.1038 /s41598-023-34755-y.

Index

About the Author

Photo by Peggy Caspari

JENNIFER CASPARI, PhD, is a licensed clinical psychologist working in a group practice at Cognitive Behavior Therapy Associates of Denver (CBT Denver). Dr. Caspari specializes in general and health psychology, delivering evidence-based psychotherapies to adults experiencing a variety of concerns. She is passionate about helping clients live full and meaningful lives, including those living with acute or chronic health conditions. Her collaborative, warm, and empathetic approach focuses on enhancing functioning, ability to engage in values-based behaviors, and overall quality of life.

Dr. Caspari views much of her role as a therapist as helping clients increase their cognitive, emotional, and behavioral flexibility to improve their well-being. She writes a Psychology Today blog, *Living Well When Your Body Doesn't Cooperate.* In her free time, she enjoys spending time with loved ones, feeling the sun on her face, listening to audiobooks while moving her body, watching cooking and baking shows, and eating delicious food. You can find her on social media: @moxie_mindset.

About North Atlantic Books

North Atlantic Books (NAB) is an independent, nonprofit publisher committed to a bold exploration of the relationships between mind, body, spirit, and nature. Founded in 1974, NAB aims to nurture a holistic view of the arts, sciences, humanities, and healing. To make a donation or to learn more about our books, authors, events, and newsletter, visit www.northatlanticbooks.com.